AIRWAY ONE

J. J. Scholze
12076 Caminito Campana
Rancho Bernardo
San Diego, CA 92128

For
George Crawley W.
With Best Wishes!
Joe Shaff

Jan '89

AIRWAY ONE

A narrative
of United Airlines
and its leaders

---

by Robert E. Johnson

Research by Adrian Delfino

ISBN: 0-915174-00-6 (Hardbound)
        0-915174-01-4 (Paperback)

Library of Congress Catalog Card Number: 74-19586

Printed and bound at *The Lakeside Press,*
R. R. Donnelley & Sons Company, Chicago, Illinois
and Crawfordsville, Indiana

Printed in the United States of America

Designed by The Spencer Group, Chicago, Illinois

To The Memory of
Harold Crary

Contents

Foreword

In the earlier years *of our company, the history of United Airlines was told in the book,* High Horizons, *by Frank J. Taylor.*

Much has happened since then, and the time has come for a new account of where our company has been, and where it may be going. Such an account should be more than historical—it should reflect the philosophies and the policies which have molded United, and which underlie its foundation.

Upon his retirement as executive vice-president and director, I asked Robert E. Johnson to undertake this mission. He is uniquely qualified to write about the company which he joined in 1929. He participated in the formation of United under the direction of Philip G. Johnson; he worked side by side with Pat Patterson for four decades; he served on George Keck's management team; and after years of personal acquaintance, he was closely associated with me during the first years of my tenure as president. On his retirement in 1972 Bob became a director emeritus and consultant to me.

One of very few persons to have served with each of United's four presidents, Bob Johnson tells how and why United Airlines fulfilled its destiny as the Free World's greatest airline.

Edward E. Carlson

Preface

Four decades *and more of deep involvement with United have made it difficult to be objective in writing about the company and its leaders. Even my desert home has such close links with Chicago that I found it hard to achieve a detached viewpoint to put this story into perspective.*

So AIRWAY ONE was written on an ocean liner, of all places, sailing across the sea reaches of the Southern Hemisphere — down the long stretches of the South Atlantic, through the remote Straits of Magellan, up the almost limitless South Pacific.

On the S. S. Santa Mariana *I did find detachment, and I am indebted to my wife, Rosalie, and to the ship's officers for making that possible. Adrian Delfino provided invaluable research assistance which I deeply appreciate. I am particularly grateful to Eddie Carlson for asking me to write his story and for giving me the freedom to say it as I saw it.*

Bob Johnson

Palm Desert, California
1974

xi

Prologue

T he 747 *traces chalky contrails across the slate-colored evening sky seven miles above the plains of Nebraska, while far below in the dusky airspace there is the memory of a bygone airway pioneered by the mail planes of the twenties. And at ground level, unseen in the darkness of the prairie, are faint ruts made by the covered wagons on their way west.*

AIRWAY ONE is the designation of the air operating certificate issued by the federal government to United. It spans the country's main route of transportation and communication, opened up more than a century ago by the pioneering scouts and settlers who crossed the continent in their prairie schooners.

This is the famed Overland Trail — the historic route of the covered wagon trains, the daring Pony Express riders, the long steel rails of the Iron Horse, and the thin wires of the first transcontinental telegraph.

This is the lifeline of our nation.

Early in the twentieth century the drama of the Overland Trail was climaxed by the pioneering airmen who flew the first coast-to-coast airmail across uncharted skies above the path of the Pony Express riders.

Today jets of many airlines speed back and forth over this historic route.

But it was United Airlines — then as now, holder of U.S. Air Certificate Number One — that alone pioneered coast-to-coast air passenger and cargo schedules over this airway.

AIRWAY ONE is the story of United Airlines, and how it grew from the nation's first coast-to-coast airline to the largest air transport system in the Free World. It is a narrative of pioneering and leadership across 50 years of flying from small propeller planes to great jetliners.

It is the saga of the people who built a record of leadership unequalled in all the world of air transportation.

Tens of thousands of United men and women have contributed to this record: the pilots who risked their lives to open the airway, and the mechanics who did their best to make the machines airworthy; the engineers who worked to improve safety; the stewardesses who symbolized friendly service; and all the many others who have made up the great United team over the years.

Every team has a leader charged with full responsibility at its final level. United has had four leaders: Presidents Philip G. Johnson, William A. Patterson, George E. Keck, and Edward E. Carlson. All four have contributed to the building of United, two especially so.

Patterson piloted United ably and dynamically through more than three decades of growth. He left an indelible stamp of quality and character on the company.

Carlson took the controls at a critical time in United's history, and he had made his mark unmistakably clear well before the end of his third year.

It is noteworthy that both men are best known throughout United's system by their nicknames, and much of this narrative is about Pat and Eddie.

AIRWAY ONE tells about the philosophies which have marked the road to United's leadership; it describes the challenges and problems which arose, and what was done about them and why; it portrays the environment in which United was born and grew to maturity.

AIRWAY ONE may be of historical interest, but its mission is to provide background to United's managers of today and its leaders of tomorrow. The events of the past 50 years are their heritage, as well as the foundation for their future years.

The Pioneering years

1926-1934

Philip G. Johnson, giant of
air transport's pioneering years and
first president of United Airlines.

The early chapters *of United Airlines' story are studded with names of great aviation pioneers.*

There were the airmen like Ham Lee, pioneer airmail pilot and for many years number one on United's seniority list, and Jack Knight, who flew the first night mail through snowswept skies.

There were the engineers like Thorp Hiscock who solved "impossible" technical problems to give those pilots navigating aids to go with the seats of their pants.

There were the entrepreneurs like Vern Gorst and Walter Varney who risked and lost their financial shirts to start the airlines that were to form United in later years.

There were far-sighted financiers like William E. Boeing who put major fortunes on the line to develop airlines and equip them with the right airplanes to operate efficiently and profitably.

And there was Philip Gustav Johnson, born in Seattle of immigrant parents from Sweden, and graduated from the University of Washington's Engineering School in 1917. When in that year the small airplane factory founded by Boeing received an order for a few military training planes, Johnson went to work helping to build those airplanes. By 1925 he was president of Boeing, and two years later he bid and got a contract with the Post Office Department to inaugurate commercial airmail service over the Chicago-San Francisco leg of the transcontinental airway, the nucleus of what was to become United Airlines.

Johnson was far more than a competent engineer. Cool, with blue eyes that could become icy in times of stress, humorous with a predilection for Swedish dialect stories, a taskmaster who worked hard and sometimes played as hard—he was above all an extremely able businessman.

Johnson became United Airlines' first president in 1931. Two years later he was promoted to the presidency of United Aircraft and Transport Corporation— one of aviation's first conglomerates, which included Boeing, Pratt & Whitney, and other companies in addition to United Airlines and its operating divisions.

In 1934 Johnson was out of a job, barred from U. S. air transportation for five years because of the so-called blacklist which followed President Roosevelt's cancellation of all airmail contracts. Johnson was not guilty of any collusion as charged, and his name was cleared years later after United had filed an appeal to the Court of Claims. The Court found that the charges of collusion had been trumped up, for United's contracts had been legal in all respects.

Exiled from the industry he had helped to found, Johnson returned to Seattle and took over a truck manufacturing company. A year later, when the Canadian government decided to establish an airline across the Dominion, it rescued Phil Johnson from the New Deal doghouse to establish its national airline. With a group of old Boeing Associates he went to Montreal, and in 18 months TransCanada Airlines (now Air Canada) was in full-scale transcontinental operation.

At the end of the five-year blacklist sentence, Johnson returned to head the Boeing Airplane Company and eventually to lead the fantastic production of Boeing B-17 "Flying Fortress" bombers which were so vital to victory in World War II. During this service to his country, Johnson died of a heart attack to close a truly great career in the pioneering years of aviation.

Chapter 1

The days of the Airmail

ince the epochal flight of the Wright Brothers, the airplane has fulfilled two roles—one of war, the other of peace. During the past seven decades, people of the world have lifted their eyes to airplanes at times in fear, at times in pride. Never has an airplane flown over the continental United States on a destructive military mission, but America did feel the impact of aerial bombing on December 7, 1941. The military mission has been progressively destructive—through the World Wars, Korea, and Viet Nam—and the airplane's strength as a deterrent has been inestimable.

But its peaceful mission has been far more significant. Perhaps no other single force can equal the airplane in its capacity to forge mutual understanding among the peoples of the world, as it makes neighbors of distant nations—bringing the peoples of the hemispheres across oceans and borders and walls to meet and to know each other. No other force has the potential to build such lasting bonds of peace.

For generations man had nurtured the dream of flight. Da Vinci drew imaginative representations of aerial vehicles, and early day balloons carried adventurers and letters on cross-country flights. The Wright Brothers launched the Air Age with their historic days at Kitty Hawk when they first achieved heavier-than-air flight.

But to some far-sighted men in Washington, D.C. goes the credit for translating the American dream of flying into the reality of regular air schedules, of converting military aircraft to peaceful pursuits. Even as the airplane intensified its combatant role in World War I—as the Rickenbackers and Richthofens were sweeping the skies across France—the planning for today's great U.S. air transport network began in the offices of the United States Post Office Department at the nation's capital.

In the wartime planes and pilots, men with vision could see the nucleus of a network of commercial air routes across the nation, carrying the commerce still bound to the land. So the Post Office Department joined with the army's Signal Corps to test the concept of scheduled airmail service. The plan was a simple one. Army pilots would fly Curtiss "Jenny" biplanes on a Washington-Philadelphia-New York route under the direction of the Post Office Department. On May 15, 1918, the service was inaugurated on the basis of a round-trip schedule each day. Thus was fulfilled a responsibility assigned to the Post Office by the Congress when it passed an "Air Mail" bill in 1910 intended to determine the feasibility of scheduled flying.

For 12 weeks the experimental service was operated across the route. During those three months, the army pilots flew 254 schedules, amounting to 29,500 miles— statistics insignificant by today's standards, but sufficiently impressive to warrant the development of scheduled air service on a permanent basis.

The men of the Post Office could not foresee that from their single daily round-trip flight between New York and the nation's capital, air traffic would grow to the point that a half-century later this eastern corridor would be the most heavily traveled air route in the world, and that in such a future time many millions of people and tons of goods would be moving across U.S. airways. But they could and did foresee a regular air route not just between New York and Washington, but between New York and San Francisco, spanning the continent, crossing the mountains and the rivers and the prairies of America.

It would take five years fully to accomplish this goal, but it would assure the future of scheduled air transportation and make the United States the world's greatest civil air power.

While the army had flown the experiment in 1918, the responsibility for the airmail service was clearly civilian, so the Post Office Department moved to accept the challenge. Many men joined in that project, but one stood out as the leader. He was Otto Praeger, assistant postmaster general, called "The Father of Air Mail." Modest and selfless, but fearless and tenacious, Praeger went to the Hill to get congressional approval for the necessary funding, and he went to the aircraft industry for the kind of planes he needed to fly the transcontinental route. He mapped the course they would fly—New York-Cleveland-Chicago-Omaha-Cheyenne-Salt Lake City-San Francisco, with intermediate airports at such places as Bellefonte, Pennsylvania; Rock Springs, Wyoming; Elko, Nevada; and many more—for his planes would need to stop every few hundred miles to refuel. He hired civilian pilots—mostly World War I veterans and county fair barnstormers—to fly his planes.

On December 12, 1918, the first leg of that transcontinental airway was attempted between New York and Chicago. Across the Allegheny Mountains three planes crashed in snowstorms, another survived a forced landing. Again, on January 2, 1919, another attempt was made with the same results.

The Alleghenies became Praeger's *bete noire*—the pilots and the press called it the "Hell Stretch" and the "Graveyard of the Air Mail." But he knew that these mountains, and the much higher Rockies and Sierras yet to be flown to the west, must not stop the airmail. With the courageous airmen who risked—and often lost—their lives, Praeger and his team persevered.

In July, 1919, New York-Chicago schedules were in operation; in May, 1920, the route had been pushed westward to Omaha, and by September, 1920, on across the Overland Trail to San Francisco. The transcontinental airway was complete, and planes were flying from the East Coast to the Pacific.

But they were flying only by day. No planes moved at night. There were no lights, no other aids to navigate in darkness. Night flying was "too perilous." The airmail was flown by day and transferred to railroads at night; and because of the delays on the ground, the combined air-rail transcontinental schedules took almost as long as all-rail service. So the cry arose—"Get a horse!"—an iron horse, that is. Railroads and others who opposed the idea of airmail stalked the Hill, and Congress was ready to write off the airmail service as a failure and vote against further appropriations.

The indomitable Otto Praeger and his brave pilots were not about to lose their two years of pioneering, so just a few weeks before the fate of the service was to be voted in Washington, they staged a melodramatic stunt.

The objective was to be a round-trip day-and-night schedule from coast to coast to demonstrate that through transcontinental airmail flying was indeed possible.

The date: February 22, 1921. Night flying in July was considered foolhardy; in February's bitter weather it seemed suicidal. But the relentless Praeger and his airmen with their vulnerable machines were determined to go ahead with this "do or die" demonstration.

The demonstration almost died—almost, but not quite. Two planes set out from New York for the West. One failed in Pennsylvania; the other was stopped at Chicago by a blizzard. Two planes started from San Francisco to the East. One crashed in Nevada; the other kept going, being flown by a relay of pilots changing at each airport.

A slim, handsome flyer, aptly named Jack Knight, flew the leg from Cheyenne to North Platte, and because a relief pilot couldn't get there he flew on to Omaha. Bonfires built by farmers at the advance request of the Post Office helped guide Knight on his way through the snowy

8

darkness to his landing at Omaha. But there he learned the eastbound flight on to Chicago was to be cancelled— blizzard conditions prevailed across Iowa and had grounded the relay pilot.

Jack Knight, tired and facing the storm to the East, climbed back into his plane and flew off into darkness, and into fame as the hero who saved the airmail.

No matter that he had never flown the route from Omaha to Chicago; he had a railroad map and a flashlight to study it in his cockpit.

No matter that the blizzard made landing at Des Moines impossible; he had enough fuel in his emergency tank to go on to Iowa City.

No matter that the ground crew at the Iowa City field, told the flight was cancelled, had gone home; a night watchman heard Knight circling in the darkness over-head and lighted a flare to guide him to a landing to fill his almost empty fuel tank.

No matter that he had snow and sleet and fog to over-come on the rest of his flight to Chicago; he landed there in the grey, cold morning to receive a true hero's welcome.

Modest and low-key, Knight said to the reporters on hand: "I happened to be the man on the spot, but any one of the rest of the fellows would have done what I did. We all knew how important this flight is, and we were all determined to make it succeed. Too many pilots have sacrificed their lives flying the mail during the past couple of years to let this thing fold up. This isn't just a case of 'the mail must go through'; the whole idea of the transcontinental airway is at stake."

Another pilot flew the mail to Cleveland, still another continued on to New York, and the first transcontinental mail flight was completed in the total elapsed time of 33 hours 20 minutes.

Otto Praeger and the pilots and ground crews had pre-vailed. Congress passed an appropriation of $1,300,000 to expand the airmail service, and to start lighting the airways and the airports.

By 1925, the transcontinental airway was completely equipped with beacons, airplanes had lighting aids installed, a weather information system was established, and around-the-clock schedules were routine.

The Post Office Department had ably fulfilled its mission to establish an airmail system—with routes beginning to extend into all parts of the country. Now the time had come to turn the airmail over to commercial operators, and plans were made to accomplish this transition through the free enterprise approach of competitive bidding.

The stage had been effectively set for the birth of the U. S. commercial air transport system, to be built by many airlines throughout the nation in partnership with the federal government. . . .

Whenever you fly across the central part of this continent, you are traveling the air trail blazed by Otto Prager's band of airmen: Ham Lee, Rube Wagner, Slim Lewis, Jack Knight, Clair Vance, Frank Yaeger, Jim Murray, Jack Eaton and scores of others who duplicated in the skies of the Overland Trail the pioneering feats of the Pony Express riders and the drivers of Ben Holladay's Overland Stage Line.

This is the legacy of Airway One—a legacy of courage and determination, a legacy of leadership.

Chapter 2

The
Pioneering
years

Beginning with Boeing

Across the top of the company service pin worn by United Airlines employees are four stars. They represent the four predecessor companies which were brought together in 1931 to form United: Boeing Air Transport, National Air Transport, Pacific Air Transport, and Varney Air Lines. The first star stands for Boeing, the principal force in the development of United Airlines. Boeing bred the men who were to lead United to first place in the Free World's air transport industry.

Boeing was William E. Boeing, who was raised in Detroit and educated at Yale's Sheffield Scientific School. He came to Seattle by acquiring extensive timber properties in western Washington, and he came to aviation by developing an interest in flying as a sport. He learned to fly in 1915 and decided he could build a better airplane than the seaplane he was then riding around in. So in 1916 he organized his aircraft company and built the better airplane, the first of tens of thousands of fine planes.

Boeing's first plane led to military contracts. The commercial market was virtually nonexistent. Building trainers and patrol planes kept the little plant busy, but Boeing did take time to build one commercial aircraft—and thus make a very early entry into air transportation. His test pilot, Edward Hubbard, persuaded Boeing to build a seaplane and seek a contract to carry foreign mail between Seattle and Victoria, British Columbia. The contract was awarded in 1920, and for the next 10 years foreign mail was flown between these ports to cut 24 hours from transpacific steamship mail delivery time between Seattle and the Orient.

In addition to Hubbard (whose interest in scheduled flying would later spur Boeing into transcontinental operations), another associate who joined Boeing in 1919 was Philip G. Johnson, the engineering graduate of the University of Washington who was to become the first president of United Airlines. Johnson served as Boeing's right-hand administrator and was responsible in great part for the company's growth through the twenties.

In February, 1925, Congress reviewed the status of the Post Office's airmail service, determined that the government's pioneering role had indeed been fulfilled, and passed the Kelly Act, which authorized the Post Office Department to negotiate the transfer of the several air mail routes to commercial operators through competitive bidding.

In its manufacturing environment, Boeing paid little attention to this action—except for Eddie Hubbard who was still running the Seattle-Victoria foreign airmail route, all 84 miles of it. Hubbard learned that in the government's plan for spinning off the domestic airmail routes, U.S. Airway Number One, the transcontinental, would be divided into segments: San Francisco-Chicago as Certificate #18; and Chicago-New York as #17. (In 1935 the entire route was united and Certificate #1 issued to United Airlines.)

Convinced that Boeing should operate commercial aircraft as well as build them, Hubbard made an analysis of the 2,000-mile California-Chicago route—schedules, expected volumes, growth projections, estimated costs and earnings. Because of the varied operating conditions, no airplane then current could perform with maximum efficiency—but one could be designed and built by Boeing. Armed with his facts and figures, Eddie Hubbard met with Boeing, Johnson, and other Boeing officers, and a

12

decision was made to bid for the San Francisco-Chicago route. This and the Chicago-New York portion of the transcontinental would be the last routes to be turned over to private contractors—in the summer of 1927, more than a year after lesser routes had been awarded.

Hubbard's proposal, refined by Johnson, was carefully worked out to provide a reasonable bottom-line profit. It was submitted at a base rate of $1.50 per pound per 1,000 miles of flying, which was about half of the next lowest bid.

Outraged cries from competitive bidders filled the skies. Boeing was charged with financial irresponsibility, of wanting an outlet for its aircraft and coming in with a cut-rate bid to get it, and with threatening the financial stability of the budding new air transport business. (This hue and cry was all but forgotten seven years later when, in Senate hearings held after the Roosevelt Administration cancelled the airmail contracts, an attempt was made to support charges of graft and collusion, and Mr. Boeing was accused of profiteering.)

In January, 1927, Boeing was awarded the San Francisco-Chicago route, and the Post Office Department had this to say:

"The financial responsibility of this company is regarded by the Postmaster General as beyond question while the practical part of the business is to be under the direction of Edward Hubbard who has flown the oldest established contract operated under the Post Office Department, between Seattle, Washington, and Victoria, thereby saving 24 hours in the dispatch and receipt of mail at the Seattle Office."

Thus, two-thirds of Airway One became Boeing's by contract, and now the legal document needed men and machines to transform it into an airline in five months. The takeover from the Post Office was scheduled for July 1, 1927.

Boeing, as chairman, named Johnson as president and Eddie Hubbard as the operations vice-president. The nucleus of flight and ground personnel was the Post Office's operating organization—the skilled pilots who had so ably pioneered that 2,000-mile stretch of skies, and the operations and mechanical people who managed the ground handling of schedules. In fact, D. B. Colyer, then superintendent of the U.S. Air Mail Service, was selected to become operations manager. (Two years later, when Eddie Hubbard died of a heart attack, Colyer succeeded him as vice-president for Boeing's airline operations.)

A tougher problem was that of aircraft. A couple of years before, Boeing had designed and built a prototype mail plane for the Post Office, but it wasn't ordered. Now the plans were dusted off, a two-passenger compartment was added, and Pratt & Whitney (later to be the foundation of United Aircraft) was requested to expedite production of "Wasp" radial engines. The Boeing factory started building 25 Model 40A planes in February. The first was completed June 1, and three weeks later all were on the line. The total price for the whole fleet was $150,000.

Between June 20 and July 1, pilots were checked out on the new planes, mechanics indoctrinated in their servicing, and on the target date Boeing Air Transport commenced flying between Chicago and San Francisco (actually Oakland, whose commercial airport served the Bay area).

Boeing's service was an immediate success, both operationally and financially, to the consternation of competitive critics who had claimed Boeing would lose its shirt on its "too low" bid. Professional operating experience, highly efficient (for that time) aircraft, and a small bonus in passenger-carrying capability added up to a comfortable amount of black ink below the line—so much so, in fact, that at the end of 1927, after only six months of operations, the directors declared a 1-3/4% dividend on preferred stock, and a $1 dividend on the common stock.

14

But the Boeing years were important to United's future system for developing more than the Chicago-San Francisco route. Another airline, started independently a year before BAT as a private contractor on the West Coast airmail segment, was made a part of the Boeing airline operation prior to the formation of United Airlines. This was Pacific Air Transport, acquired in January, 1928.

In addition, Varney Air Lines, operating in the western United States between Portland and Salt Lake City, would later fit well into Boeing's expanding system.

A pioneering entrepreneur named Vern Gorst, a resident of Coos Bay, Oregon, who operated some motor stage lines in the Pacific Northwest, founded Pacific Air Transport in January, 1926. Gorst had developed a yen for flying in 1925, learned to fly, bought a flying boat, and was undismayed when he cracked it up in a few months. He was convinced that someday the airplane would lure passengers away from the bus and the train. So when he learned the Post Office was going to establish a new airmail route along the Pacific Coast to be awarded through competitive bidding, Gorst went into action. He got some stage line associates and others to pledge financial backing, and he submitted a bid for the new route.

His bid was accepted; it was the only one submitted.

Unlike the transcontinental route, this segment had not been operated as an airway, and preparations for starting service on September 15, 1926, took some doing. Prospective landing sites were surveyed, and airway beacons were improvised with automobile headlights mounted on revolving bases. For air navigation by daylight, Gorst persuaded the Standard Oil Company to paint the names of towns on the tops of its numerous gasoline stations.

For aircraft, Gorst and his chief pilot, Grover Tyler, selected Ryan monoplanes similar to the type Lindbergh flew across the Atlantic.

Gorst's operation was pretty much a shoestring. Many

of his airplanes were lost in crashes, and new and larger aircraft were needed. He had two sources for obtaining capital—selling stock to friends, and borrowing from banks. He did both, and in pursuit of the latter course, he went into the Wells Fargo Bank in San Francisco one day. It was noon, and the senior loan officers were out to lunch. Gorst approached W. A. Patterson, a young assistant cashier in his twenties. Gorst needed money and didn't have much security, but Patterson spent enough time with him to see the potential of a new and exciting business. He authorized a $5,000 loan. He went on to serve as an unpaid financial advisor to Gorst, and ultimately was instrumental in arranging a favorable merger for PAT with Boeing in 1928. This was good for Gorst for it provided the capital required for the development of the route, and it assured that all of PAT's employees would be kept on the payroll (30 years later this employee protection clause became a historic industry precedent in United's acquisition of Capital). The merger was good for Boeing because the company was able to cross its transcontinental "tee" with the strategic coastwise route. It was good for the West Coast cities involved because Boeing substantially upgraded the quality of service.

And the merger was mutually good for Patterson and the future of United Airlines because it brought the two together. For the following year Patterson took the position of assistant to Johnson, then president of both the Boeing manufacturing and operating companies. When Patterson talked with Frederick Lipman, then Wells Fargo president, about his decision to leave the bank, Lipman said: "You may be doing the right thing, but again you may be making a mistake; and if so, I want you to know your desk will be here for the next three years." Patterson often went back to the Wells Fargo, but he never went back to his desk.

Like Vern Gorst, Walter T. Varney was a venturesome entrepreneur, already active in aviation when the

16

Post Office began advertising airmail routes for bids. Varney was a World War I pilot and was operating a flying school and air taxi service in California. A new line had been projected from Pasco, Washington, to Elko, Nevada, via Boise, Idaho. Two more unlikely terminal points could not have been selected, but the idea was to fly mail from Pasco, a railroad division point, to Elko, the nearest connection with the transcontinental airmail service as the crow flew. Unfortunately the route covered a hazardous and desolate stretch of 460 miles, and no one took the Post Office seriously when it invited new airline operators to compete for the Pasco-Elko contract. No one, that is, except Varney.

With his flying instructor, Leon Cuddeback, Varney drove back and forth across the mountains, the wheatlands, and the deserts that separated Elko from Pasco, and he was convinced the route was feasible. They filed their bid, and inasmuch as it was the only one, it was accepted forthwith.

Varney started its schedules on April 6, 1926, with a fleet of new Swallow mail planes, underpowered with World War I type engines. The inaugural flight was piloted from Pasco to Elko with a stop at Boise. It went according to the timetable, and all was well. The opposite flight that day and all the flights for the next two days were plagued with engine failures and had to be aborted. Varney asked for and received government permission to suspend operations for 60 days. During the interim the airplanes had new, more powerful engines installed. When service was resumed on June 6, everything went well.

This episode has led to some friendly feuding between United and Western Airlines. United says it is the oldest airline in the U.S., hanging its claim on the April 6, 1926, date. Western, which started its Los Angeles-Salt Lake City route on April 15, 1926, and continued without interruptions, claims *it* is the nation's oldest airline, arguing that Varney's April 6 inaugural doesn't count. United ignores Western's argument, pointing out that after all it did start scheduled service between Pasco and Elko nine days before Western. And then there are those on both sides of the competitive fence who feel it really doesn't make much difference anyway, that anybody who's been running an airline since 1926—no matter what day of what month—is pretty old and knows all there is to know about running an airline.

In early 1930 Varney decided to get out of the airline and go back to California, where he started up a short-lived airline between San Francisco and Los Angeles. Later that year Boeing would acquire the pioneer Varney operation in the Pacific Northwest.

Thus, when United Airlines was formed in 1931, three of its four-star companies—Boeing, PAT, and Varney—were in the West, accounting for 70 percent of what would be its basic routes.

The fourth was National Air Transport, representing the essential Chicago-New York segment of the transcontinental route, along with an airway between Chicago and Texas.

Airway One could not be complete without National Air Transport. Adding the fourth star became crucially important.

Chapter 3

Next came NAT

F**or years** the transportation link between New York and Chicago has been one of the primary traffic arteries in the world. During the first two decades of this century, railroads had heavily developed this route; two were dominant—the New York Central with its flag train, "The 20th Century Limited," and the Pennsylvania with its "Broadway Limited."

So this segment of the original Post Office transcontinental airway was indeed a plum, both for its own potential and as the vital eastern link of the coast-to-coast route. A group of eastern and midwestern businessmen decided to organize an airline to obtain the airmail contract for this segment, and formed National Air Transport in May, 1925. Leading this move were Clement Keys, a New York investment banker, and Howard Coffin, Detroit automobile official, and Col. Paul Henderson, former assistant postmaster general, who was named general manager of the new company. Efforts were made to include Edsel Ford, heading the Ford Company's interest in aircraft manufacture (the Stout metal plane which would lead to the famed Ford Trimotor) and airline operation (the Chicago-Detroit-Cleveland route), but these efforts failed. (However, a spin-off of the Ford operation, Stout Air Services, was later acquired by United.)

Well organized and adequately financed, NAT was all set to go after the New York-Chicago route by the time the Post Office was to call for airmail contract bids. The only problem was when the Post Office did so in July, 1925, the New York-Chicago route was not included—it would be delayed for more than a year. The new airline had no place to go except to bid on another route, selecting the Chicago-Kansas City-Dallas airway as important in offering a direct connection with the hoped for New York-Chicago line at a future time.

On May 12, 1926, NAT inaugurated airmail schedules on its new route and became the second oldest predecessor division of United, antedated only by Varney.

Then early in 1927, New York-Chicago bids were invited by the government, and NAT was successful in obtaining this contract. And as the company prepared to inaugurate this service, its president, Howard Coffin, most effectively prophesied the new role of commercial air transportation in an April, 1927, memorandum to NAT's Board of Directors:

"This company was organized for the purpose of operating an air transport service between New York and Chicago. Other activities with which the NAT has concerned itself since its incorporation have been incident to or preparatory for the consummation of this original plan. We find ourselves in position to devote our undivided attention to the achievement of that important national service toward which the energies of our organization have been, since the beginning, directed. We have a sizable job on our hands.

"It is intimately related, upon the one hand, to our National Defense, and upon the other, to a still greater speeding up of those business processes of communication and transportation directly affecting the economic welfare of our country of vast distances and widely scattered commercial interests. The picture as to future possibilities can well be left to your own lively imaginations."

On September 1, 1927, NAT commenced its schedules between New York and Chicago, connecting there with

Boeing's service west to San Francisco. Thus was completed the nation's first commercial coast-to-coast air service; but like the precedent of the railroads, two different companies operated the two separate segments of that airway.

NAT's headquarters were located in Chicago, Boeing Air Transport's in Seattle. BAT carried passengers from San Francisco to Chicago; NAT carried only mail from Chicago to New York, although it did transport passengers between Chicago and Dallas/Fort Worth. The latter route crossed flat, open country, while the eastern segment spanned the Alleghenies, which maintained their reputation as the "Hell Stretch."

Still, there were a few adventurers who wanted to travel by air across the continent. They would ride in the discomfort of a small compartment in BAT's Boeing 40B, at a ticket price of $200 from San Francisco to Chicago. When they could persuade NAT to accommodate them on a flight on to the east, they would be outfitted with parachute, helmet, and goggles, and sit on top of sacks of letters in the open mail compartment of NAT's mail plane for the trip from Chicago to New York, also at a ticket price of $200. The elapsed time of such an expedition from California to New York was about 34 hours of continuous air travel.

The notion that attempting to carry passengers across the Allegheny Mountains was too hazardous continued to be an obsession with NAT (although some believe another reason for NAT's dim view of the passenger business was that carrying the mail was considerably more profitable and a lot less bother). This led NAT into a unique air-rail experiment that for a time threatened a prospective future marriage with BAT.

The fertile-minded Clement Keys, a director and chairman of NAT's executive committee, was deeply involved in various aviation enterprises, and he was a strong factor in Eastern Air Transport, Curtiss Flying Services, and Curtiss Airports. One of the more interesting of such activities was TAT—Transcontinental Air Transport—organized by Keys and others in 1928 to operate air-rail passenger service across the country. Travelers would move from New York to Columbus via the Pennsylvania Railroad (to avoid those mountains), then fly in TAT's Ford Trimotors from Columbus to Waynoka, Oklahoma; then they would board the Santa Fe for an overnight run to Clovis, New Mexico, and there hop on another TAT airplane for the last lap to Los Angeles. The process was simply reversed for eastbound travelers. The elapsed time was about 48 hours for the coast-to-coast trip.

NAT, through Keys, participated in the formation and early operation of TAT. In fact, NAT's chief operating officer, Col. Henderson, donned a TAT hat and served as operating head of that company as well. His presence was somewhat overshadowed by another associate, for Keys retained Charles Lindbergh as technical advisor. TAT was promoted as "The Lindbergh Line," and Lindbergh was active and instrumental in its operating affairs.

The chief engineer for TAT was J. A. "Jack" Herlihy, M. I. T. graduate and navy pilot. He was later to become a pilot for National Air Transport, and then for many years was senior vice-president of engineering and maintenance for United Airlines.

NAT was involved in other activities as well, including local flying services for sightseeing, air taxi, and charter flights. But nothing was as important and as successful as its own airline operation. And no amount of reluctance to fly people across the "Hell Stretch" and no effort to sell the idea of a 48-hour air-rail service could do more than delay NAT's destiny to become a most vital part of a single all-air operation across the continent.

Before this could happen, there would be a financial and legal battle over the airline, but ultimately destiny would prevail and NAT would become the fourth star in United's crown, while TAT would gradually evolve into one of United's principal competitors—TWA.

Chapter 4

United we fly

U nited **Airlines** comes from Seattle, although its
official home has always been Chicago. Three of
the four men who have served as its chief executive were developed in Seattle. Most of the airplanes it
flies were built there.

United Airlines was formally launched in 1931, the
result of a circuitous and complex chain of corporate
events that began in the Seattle headquarters of Boeing,
by then the nation's largest airplane factory and the operator of two airlines.

The airlines needed new and larger aircraft, and the
Boeing factory was on the verge of important new military contracts. William Boeing had already invested
much of his personal fortune in his enterprises, and he
felt it was time to seek major outside financing. This
wouldn't be difficult, for investors were discovering aviation in the exciting aftermath of Lindbergh's flight to
Paris.

Riding the 1928 crest of the bull market, financiers had
been putting the young aviation industry through a series
of corporate acquisitions and mergers that had already
resulted in three significant conglomerates:

The Keys' group included National Air Transport and
the other companies that later spawned TWA and Eastern Airlines.

The second was a loose organization put together by
Fokker Aircraft and General Motors, with some airlines

in the West that ended up as Western Airlines.

Aviation Corporation was the third conglomerate, and the airlines drawn into this organization developed into American Airlines.

Boeing and his associates formed Boeing Airplane & Transport Corporation late in 1928 and looked to the East for expansion. He found an aggressive partner in Frederick B. Rentschler who had organized the Pratt & Whitney Aircraft Engine organization that developed the famous "Wasp" engine for Boeing's first mail planes.

With Rentschler and Pratt & Whitney, Boeing added the Vought Airplane & Hamilton Propeller companies. In early 1929 the group was renamed the United Aircraft and Transport Corporation, with Boeing as chairman and Rentschler as president. They continued their expansion drive, adding the Sikorsky and Stearman Aircraft companies and Stout Air Service. The Stout acquisition was particularly interesting. William B. Stout had designed and built an all-metal airplane (unique at that time) which attracted the attention of Edsel Ford. As a result, Stout was brought in to head up the airplane division of Ford Motor Company, which built the famous Ford Trimotor and operated air routes between Detroit-Chicago and Detroit-Cleveland. When Ford lost interest in aviation, United Aircraft & Transport Corporation bought the Stout Air Service.

By now the stage was set for the most important and difficult acquisition of all—National Air Transport.

Keys had the vital New York-Chicago route of NAT, and was striving for a West Coast presence by acquiring substantial interests in Varney Air Lines and Western Air Express, serving the Southwest.

United Aircraft made an effort to negotiate a merger directly with the NAT subsidiary of Keys, but this was blocked. Then United Aircraft turned to the direct approach of acquiring control of National Air Transport's stock, precipitating a bitter corporate struggle with Keys in early 1930. After a series of ploys and counterploys with proxy battles and court actions, United Aircraft emerged with control in April, 1930.

On the heels of the NAT victory, United Aircraft turned its attention to Varney, now operating the route from Salt Lake City to Portland, Seattle and Spokane, and by June, 1930, the basic structure of the United Airlines-to-be was complete.

New equipment, new standards of passenger service, new routes, and new corporate acquisitions all posed problems of coordination. While corporate policies were developed for the subsidiaries by United Aircraft & Transport Corporation out of its New York headquarters, such policies were implemented independently by each of the subsidiaries. Too often, the arrangement gave rise to duplication of efforts among members of the United family. At other times, the lack of close communication between subsidiaries resulted in wasted projects, such as Pratt & Whitney developing engines much too large for any Boeing aircraft in the production or design stage.

It was this situation which led to the formation on March 27, 1931, of United Airlines, Inc., at first purely a management company which contracted to provide management services for each of the airline subsidiaries it was to unite. The new company would coordinate policies of management, operation, and accounting among the air transport subsidiaries and serve as a common agency for the purchase of equipment and supplies and the placing of advertising and insurance. Apart from achieving operational efficiency, the airline subsidiaries looked for economic gains from the arrangement. While United Airlines could not profit under terms of the contract, its expenses were fully reimbursed by the airline subsidiaries under a prorated formula based on the percentage of each carrier's monthly mileage and gross revenues to the total monthly mileage and gross revenues of the airlines as a group.

On July 1, 1931, United Airlines established its headquarters in Chicago's LaSalle-Wacker Building and opened up for business. Its chief executive was Philip G. Johnson, and his assistant was W. A. Patterson.

Thus was evolved the first divisional concept in United, with the four operating companies—Boeing, NAT, PAT, and Varney—each conducting its own airline operations autonomously, under management policies formulated by the corporate management of United. (In 1933 Varney was merged into Boeing Air Transport, resulting in three divisions, not too different in geographic layout from the present three-divisional operating structure.)

One of the first system-wide problems to require attention was new equipment. Each operating company had its own aircraft types—single-engine Boeing 40B's, trimotored Boeing 80A's, Ford trimotors and the like. New and better airplanes were needed, and United had a unique opportunity to standardize its fleet.

In 1932 a fleet of 59 new-type Boeing 247 airplanes powered with Pratt & Whitney "Wasp" engines was ordered. The airplane was then radical in design: a low-wing all-metal monoplane with a then-novel retractable landing gear and a cruising speed of 160 miles per hour. Its top speed was 180 miles per hour, permitting its promotion as the nation's first three-mile-a-minute passenger plane. It carried ten passengers, felt to be the optimum size for an airliner in view of the evident need for frequency of schedules. (The Boeing chief engineer at that time predicted the 247 would be the largest transport plane ever built.)

Its cost was $68,000 per unit, so the fleet of 59 represented a capital outlay of around $4,000,000 (less than today's price of one relatively small Boeing 727).

There was no looking around at other manufacturers' designs, no comparative aircraft evaluations, no competitive bidding. This was an "in-house" United Aircraft project.

For one year United Airlines had a field day with the

fastest, most modern service in the sky. And with its fleet order tying up Boeing's production line, no competitor could get its hands on a 247 until United received delivery of its 59th plane, sometime in 1934.

The rosy picture turned grey in 1934 when TWA showed up with the 14-passenger Douglas DC-2, and it became darker in 1935 when American started operating the 21-passenger DC-3. Overnight United's 247 had become the smallest, slowest, noisiest airliner in the competitive air of the Big Three and to make matters worse, it had a unique and most undesirable cabin feature—a wing spar that protruded right through the cabin and annoyed passengers and stewardesses alike as they clambered over it going up and down the aisle.

Characteristically, United chose to ignore its competitive equipment disadvantage, and it struck a very positive public image. "We promoted and sold the Boeing 247 as aggressively as we could," Sales Vice-president Harold Crary said a few years later. One advertisement depicted a 247 speeding through starlit midnight skies with the brash headline: "Swift and silent as the night!" But no amount of positive sales power could long delay the exodus of air travelers from the 247's to the larger, quieter, and faster DC-3's.

So the company learned an early and bitter lesson in technical obsolescence. Then a startling development occurred in 1934 to change the equipment procurement picture drastically, and for the better. This was the airmail contract cancellation, which was to shake up the whole air transport industry.

Before this however, organizational changes were being shaped that would have a profound effect upon the company's future. The reorganization began with a plan to unify the operating divisions, eliminating their corporate entities and converting United Airlines from a management to a full-fledged operating company. In anticipation of this, Johnson was elected to the presidency of United Aircraft and Transport Corporation in 1933, and

Patterson, by this time vice-president of United Airlines, became its president. But the reorganization of United and its operating companies was never executed by its parent holding company. Instead, it was dramatically forced into being by the federal government in early 1934.

Walter Folger Brown, a Toledo attorney, was appointed postmaster general by President Hoover in 1929. When he took inventory of his departmental responsibilities, he found an interesting situation in the country's airmail service. First, there was a crazy-quilt network of airmail contract routes that lacked any reasonable pattern—a situation that put into focus a problem that still exists in the airline industry 45 years later. Quite simply, there was no basic national airline route plan (and there was still none in 1974). Second, he found that there was no effective element of competitive routes among the carriers. Third, it became evident that without some incentive not then present, the carriers would not push for improvement in passenger service which was only a small revenue factor compared with mail contract income.

Brown was responsible for legislation being enacted to provide premium mail pay for technical improvements such as radio and aids to night flying—for this would improve the service to the public. He also initiated, through congressional action, premium rates of mail pay for passenger seats in mail planes—for this would make carriers less dependent upon mail pay and reduce airmail costs to the taxpayer. (In 1929 airmail accounted for 95 percent of airline revenues; in 1974 airmail accounted for 5 percent of airline revenues.)

Then Brown turned his attention to the hodge podge of air routes. He initiated revisions to increase long haul scheduling. He introduced competitive routes where there were none. He put pressure on small carriers to merge with large ones to strengthen and stabilize the route system. United was not a beneficiary of these route manipulations; all it received was a short run from Omaha to Watertown, South Dakota, which it didn't want and later dropped, and a 100-mile extension of its West Coast route from Los Angeles to San Diego.

To accomplish these objectives, which in his mind, and in fact, were responsive to the public convenience and necessity, Brown held a meeting at Washington with airline officials in May, 1930, to tell them what he intended to make them do to obtain air certificates for the existing airmail contracts. This was pretty much a one-way conference, and while United's president and some other company officers attended the session, they had nothing to say for the simple reason United wasn't materially involved in the big airway network reshapement. There were subsequent meetings which United did not bother to attend.

A news reporter named Fulton Lewis learned of Brown's meetings, spent much of a year digging into the story, and passed his report along to William Randolph Hearst, who put it in the files unpublished. Meanwhile, a Senate committee headed by Hugo Black was set up in September, 1933, to investigate steamship and airmail contracts. Senator Black learned of the Fulton Lewis report on Brown's contract-handling methods and successfully pressed Hearst for a copy, which fueled the committee's investigation. By that time, the then incumbent Postmaster General James Farley was receiving reports from his general counsel on the situation, which suggested Brown had resorted to conspiracy and collusion with air carrier executives to eliminate free and competitive air route certificate awards. Acting on such reports, President Roosevelt didn't wait for the Black Committee to reach its findings. He simply directed Postmaster General Farley to cancel the airmail contracts.

All airmail contracts were thus cancelled on February 9, 1934. The President asked General Benjamin Foulois, chief of the Army Air Corps, if army pilots could fly the mail, and the answer was "yes." It should have been "no." But the army started flying mail on February 20.

The results were frightful. Untrained for the rough weather and night flying that the airline pilots had conducted since the days of the U.S. Air Mail Service, and unfamiliar with the routes that traversed hazardous mountain ranges, the military flyers boldly launched their operations, using army aircraft that were hardly suitable for carrying mail. February, traditionally a difficult month for flying, was particularly bad that year. Winter freeze and snowstorms gripped much of the country, and by the end of the first week, five military pilots had been killed and six more critically injured in accidents that wiped out half a million dollars' worth of army aircraft. Reducing the operations to daylight hours only did not relieve the situation. Where transcontinental mail had taken 19 hours to travel in commercial aircraft, it took the army two days to fly the mail across the country. And still the accidents continued to pile up.

By April, twelve army pilots had died in crashes, nine of them losing their lives flying United's routes.

Public outrage, once directed at the airlines charged with collusion, profiteering, and interference with free competition, was turned to President Roosevelt who was forced to end one of the unhappier episodes in the history of air transportation. He instructed Postmaster General Farley to invite bids on new mail contracts, stressing that none of the airlines or their top executives who participated in Brown's May, 1930, "Spoils Conference" could bid on the new contracts.

On March 30, 1934, the Post Office advertised for new bids on most of the pre-cancellation routes. United Airlines, the management corporation, was ruled by the Post Office Department to be eligible to bid, providing three of its officials who had participated in the "Spoils Conference" withdrew from the company. They were Johnson, Colonel Paul Henderson, vice-president and director, and George S. Wheat, director. They were forced to resign, much to the regret of their associates.

When Pat Patterson had received word of the cancellation, which would automatically cost United most of its revenues, he telephoned every station on the system that the company's operation would be continued without curtailment or layoffs. He knew this would cost the company losses of $300,000 per month—big in those days when United's size was only 1,400 employees—but he was determined to maintain United's operations intact.

In April, 1934, Patterson submitted United's bid for its routes that had been cancelled, at the same rates in the previous contracts. It was awarded all the routes except one—the Chicago-Kansas City-Dallas airway of NAT, which went to Braniff on an extremely low bid. (Not too much later, Braniff petitioned for—and received—an increase in rate to the pre-cancellation level.)

On June 12, 1934, Congress passed the Air Mail Act of 1934 which, among other things, prohibited persons holding air mail contracts from having any financial interest in any other aviation enterprise. This signalled the end of the United Aircraft & Transport Corporation, and the other air conglomerates. The Act gave the airlines until December 31, 1934, to sever corporate ties with their aircraft, engine, propeller and various component subsidiaries.

At United Aircraft, Joseph P. Ripley, the New York financial wizard who had helped organize Boeing Airplane & Transport Corporation and was instrumental in bringing the various corporations together to form United Aircraft & Transport Corporation, was again drafted to unscramble the United family. Ripley headed a reorganization committee that included Johnson and Joseph F. McCarthy, secretary and comptroller of United Aircraft.

The organization committee was faced with a massive task—to disperse the various subsidiary companies and regroup them in a logical arrangement that would yield maximum profitability and operating efficiency. Assets of the holding company had to be distributed fairly, and its liabilities similarly disposed of.

On May 14, 1934, the board of directors of United Aircraft & Transport Corporation approved the proposed plan of reorganization for the holding company and its subsidiaries. Under the plan, three new corporations were to be formed. One of these was United Airlines Transport Corporation, which was to be formed by combining BAT, PAT, NAT, Varney, United Airlines (the management corporation) and United Airports Company of California (operating Union Air Terminal at Burbank). Another was United Aircraft Corporation, which was to be formed through merger of the Pratt & Whitney Aircraft Company, the Hamilton Standard Propeller Corporation, Northrop Aircraft Corporation, Sikorsky Aviation Corporation, United Aircraft Exports, Inc., and the United Airports of Connecticut, Inc. The third corporation was the Boeing Airplane Company, which was to be formed by combining Boeing Aircraft Company and the Stearman Aircraft Company. Functionally, the plan reflected a grouping of the air transport companies, the western manufacturing subsidiaries and the eastern manufacturing group.

For the next several months, the reorganization committee went about its task of unscrambling the empire that Boeing and Rentschler had so boldly put together. Ratios for the exchanges of stock were computed and both assets and liabilities prorated among the new corporations. Finally, on August 31, 1934, United Aircraft & Transport Corporation was put into dissolution.

In summary, the airmail contract cancellation had accomplished the following:

It subjected the airlines to a severe dislocation during their difficult, formative years. In the case of United under Patterson's leadership, the experience was the company's first real test under fire, and it did emerge stronger and wiser.

It subjected the Army Air Corps to an unfair and costly experience.

It subjected many airline pioneers—including United's great Johnson—to being blackballed from participation in the industry they had helped to found.

The airline officers may not have been guilty of collusion and conspiracy as charged. Certainly in United's case this was so, and Patterson had the company press a suit against the United States for damages caused by "illegal cancellation of its contracts." On December 7, 1942, the United States Court of Claims awarded United $364,423 for losses incurred as a result of the airmail contract cancellation.

There was a positive result of the affair—the breaking up of the large aviation holding companies. United Airlines became independent, free to make its own plans and to seek its own destiny. It would no longer be required to purchase Boeing-built planes exclusively. It could deal in aviation's competitive marketplaces, and make decisions in its own best interests.

Significantly, United's very first equipment purchase in its new freedom was for Douglas DC-3's to overcome the disadvantage of its Boeing 247's. More significantly, United was ultimately to become again Boeing's largest airline customer.

United Airlines would maintain this independence for three-and-one-half decades, until becoming a wholly owned subsidiary of UAL, Inc., in 1969.

The Patterson years

1934-1965

Pat Patterson *did more to build United Airlines than anyone else, and the company's strength today is a monument to his many attributes of leadership.*

He often observed that had the pioneers of air transportation been starting out today to blaze the air trails, there would be no airline industry, in the face of the monumental obstacles and risks which would have to be overcome. But, of course, the pioneers did take the risks and overcame the seemingly insuperable obstacles because they had the vision and the courage and the determination to identify a new frontier and to develop it.

Patterson brought to United a rare combination of abilities and talents. Some were unique, some contradictory:

Boldness: No matter how much vision and courage a leader may have, he must also have a degree of unadulterated boldness to take the occasional necessary step into the darkness of the unknown, and Pat was bold indeed. Some said his boldness was egoism typically present in men of his small stature; others simply concluded he was born that way, irrespective of size. How he got to be bold is unimportant; the fact is, boldness was a Patterson trait, and it was an asset.

Caution: For a bold leader to be cautious is not a contradiction, for there is a time to act boldly and there is a time for restraint. Pat inherited the Scotch blood of his father's ancestry—along with the warmth and bold-

ness of his mother's Portuguese sires — and he was masterful in exercising caution when caution was required. Strongly impetuous — sometimes too much so — Pat only seemed to act impulsively at times, for he usually "looked before he leaped."

Perceptiveness: He had the advantage of extraordinary perception, giving him the ability to diagnose people and problems very rapidly and usually very accurately. He possessed a sixth sense, smelling out evasions and troubles and difficulties with deadly precision no matter how well concealed they might have been. Thus he rarely stumbled over unforeseen snags.

Curiosity: Pat had a very well developed "curiosity bump" and he was able to satisfy it completely, in a variety of ways. This gave him the advantage not only of knowing what was going on, but far more important, of knowing his business and what would happen well beforehand. His consuming curiosity about all people and all things in the company and throughout the industry gave him the knowledge to lead. Few airline managers were his equal in his command of what was going on, and why.

Coolness of Judgment: Blessed with a much-better-than-average amount of common sense, Pat put knowledge and growing experience together with good judgment in most of his major decisions. He liked to hear the pros and cons and to evaluate his options (this usually didn't take very long), and then to make his decisions coolly and firmly. Once made, they usually stood up, for Pat consistently had strong convictions. On some occasions his impulsiveness would prevail over cool judgment, and later he would have to change an opinion or a stand, but his average was very good.

Business Acumen: Along with his native wit, his years at Wells Fargo in San Francisco had given Pat an excellent grounding in practical business and finance. As the business grew and more and more became involved in major financing of its expansion, United enjoyed an unusual advantage from Pat's banking background.

Sensitivity to People: Pat had a sincere and deep regard for people—those associated with him in United, those with whom he did business, in fact most people. His instinct for good personnel relations and his outgoing warmth generated a tremendous response from United employees, and built a remarkable spirit of pride and loyalty throughout the company, an invaluable resource during United's climb to leadership. His sensitivity to the customer established United as the airline of quality service, and preempted the "Friendly Skies" for United. Pat was supersensitive to his relations with others, and if someone failed the confidence placed in him or in some fashion appeared to go in some unapproved direction, Pat's warmth would quickly turn to cold disfavor, a not infrequent occurrence; and in such circumstances Pat's memory was elephantine.

Competitiveness: Born a competitor, working his way through boyhood education, possessed of strong ambition, extraordinarily quick of mind, and inherently very proud, Pat was a thoroughly competitive person; and his competitive spirit was a key part of the company's drive to industry leadership.

Those were some facets of Patterson the man. There were many others—humorous and witty, friendly, energetic, impatient, critical, short-tempered—an inventory of personal traits could be long. But those basic factors fused into his consummate skill as a leader. They represented the ingredients necessary to an entrepreneur—for he was indeed that. They made him the right man for United, and at the right time.

He served as chief executive officer of United Airlines for 33 years. In that time the company grew from a few small airmail lines to the largest airline in the Free World.

In that time the company grew to greatness.

Chapter 5

The rule of five

During its growth to maturity United Airlines had been guided by an operating code of ethics called the "Rule of Five." It began as the "Rule of Three": Safety, Passenger Comfort, Dependability. These were the operational priorities, and the company's whole organization was imbued with them. The code was then expanded to the "Rule of Five"—Honesty and Sincerity were added as goals of individual and corporate conduct.

The "Rule of Five" was conceived by Patterson as one of many ways to help mold the character and the integrity of the company he was to lead for the greater part of its first 50 years.

Johnson had been the founding force which brought United into being, and Patterson had worked at Johnson's side during those beginning years and even then strongly influenced the direction of the company.

Others were ultimately to succeed him, but in his three decades of service Pat Patterson stamped his hallmark indelibly upon United and his leadership will long be of priceless benefit to the company.

Patterson was instrumental in forming United Airlines well before he had any thought of quitting a banking career to enter the airline business.

Until he was 27 years old he had never had anything to do with airplanes. The only travel he had ever done was on a slow boat from his birthplace in Hawaii to San Francisco, and he hadn't been impressed with that experience. He was then 13 years old, the son of a Scotch-Irish manager of the Waipahu Sugar plantation and a mother of Portuguese descent. His father died when Pat was quite young, and his mother placed him in a military school while she sought ways in San Francisco to earn a living. He had inherited his mother's Latin warmth and his father's canny Scotch judgment, so that usually his emotional impulses were counterbalanced with pragmatic hardheadedness. But teen-age life in the confining military school aroused his emotions to the point that he ran away to Honolulu's harbor and joined the ship's company of the sugar schooner "Annie Johnson" as cabin boy to sail to San Francisco. Twenty-three seasick days later, he was reunited with his mother, vowing never to put to sea again, and pushing transportation into the distant background of whatever thoughts about a career he might have.

When he was 15 and graduated from grammar school, Patterson got a job as office boy at the Wells Fargo Bank, but went to night school to further his education; he completed the equivalent of high school and three years of college courses, and by the time he was 27 years old, he was assistant to a Wells Fargo vice-president, and well along in a banking career. It was then that Vern Gorst, the founder of Pacific Air Transport, came into the bank to seek the loan from Wells Fargo.

While Patterson had no interest in transportation, his imaginative mind's eye saw far beyond the flimsy planes of Gorst's PAT fleet. His vision of a future in the air may not have been as creative as that of Alfred Lord Tennyson, who wrote these prescient words in 1842:

For I dip't into the future,
Far as human eye could see,
Saw the vision of the world
And all the wonders that would be;

Saw the heavens fill with commerce,
Argosies of magic sails,
Pilots of the purple twilight,
Dropping down with costly bales . . .

These words would serve as Patterson's inspiration in later years to guide United through skies both sunny and stormy. He placed the Tennyson quotation in the lobby of United's first headquarters building, and it is reproduced in the executive suite of today's much larger corporate base.

Tennyson's prophetic promise would have made little impression on Wells Fargo's president who expressed doubt about his young employee's judgment in loaning money to someone in the flying machine business, and who advised Patterson to keep a close eye on Gorst in an effort to get the bank's money back. Patterson did watch to see the loan was repaid, and in that process changed his job from assistant to a bank president in San Francisco to assistant to Philip Johnson in Seattle.

Much of Johnson's time had been diverted from managing the production of airplanes by the Boeing Airplane Company, to the development and operation of the Boeing-owned airlines, so he was looking for a capable assistant to step in at his side.

Johnson and Patterson made a good team, meshing their opposite personalities and instincts—Johnson cool, succinct, methodical, hard-nosed; Patterson warm, outgoing, quick, imaginative. Johnson quickly gained confidence in Pat's ability and administrative energy, and gave him increasing responsibilities, particularly with the airline end of the business. So Pat was off and running, and he soon began to shape the fledgling airline for future greatness.

Pat often observed that his first major decision was to keep the airline running when the airmail contracts were abruptly cancelled by the Roosevelt Administration in 1934. From the standpoint of risk, undoubtedly he was correct. But his first major decision was made four years earlier, when he committed United—and the international airline industry—to a unique and extraordinarily effective concept of service: the air stewardess.

Prior to 1930, the scant chores of in-flight service were handled by the copilots of the early-day cabin type planes. Periodically they would leave the cockpit and pass out sandwiches and hot coffee to customers in the cabins. This was poor service at the expense of the copilot's cockpit duties. Early in 1930, Ellen Church, a nurse at San Francisco's French Hospital who had become interested in aviation, dropped in to see Steve Stimpson—Boeing Air Transport's San Francisco traffic manager—with the suggestion that the airline add a flying nurse to the crews of the transport planes to serve food and otherwise keep the passengers comfortable and happy, and her nurse's training would be a plus in the event of illness aloft. Stimpson thought the idea was great and promptly relayed the suggestion by telegram to his traffic boss—another official named W. A. Patterson who was known as "Big Pat" because of his height compared with the airline's new assistant president. Stimpson received a prompt one-word reply: "No." Undaunted (and unconcerned about channels of communication) and aware of "Little Pat's" imagination and interest in new ideas, Steve fired off this wire to the assistant president's office at Seattle:

"It strikes me that there would be a great psychological punch in having young women stewardesses or couriers, or whatever you want to call them, and I am certain that there are some mighty good ones available. I have in mind a couple of graduate nurses that would make exceptional stewardesses. Of course, it would be distinctly understood that there would be no reference made to their hospital training or nursing experience, but it would be a mighty fine thing to have this available, sub rosa, if necessary for airsickness. Imagine the psychology of having young women as regular members of the crew.

Imagine the national publicity we could get from it, and the tremendous effect it would have on the traveling public. And imagine the value they would be to us not only in the neater methods of serving food, but in looking out for the passengers' welfare.''

The decision was made by Patterson to go ahead. He authorized Stimpson and Ellen Church—who became BAT's (and the world's) first stewardess—to hire, train, and put into service eight air stewardesses on the Chicago-San Francisco flights of BAT. Ellen Church's idea, packaged with Stimpson's enthusiasm, was an immediate success. Patterson's decision was to create a new air profession that would result in hundreds of thousands of stewardesses serving the air travelers of the world— American, European, Russian, Chinese: all the airlines of the world in time followed suit. (So did railroads and buses after a while.)

His decision was a major one for an even more important reason: the air stewardess established a new concept of customer service. She became the symbol of a personal quality then lacking in surface transportation, and until then, in pioneering airline operations. Patterson saw this potential in the concept of the stewardess—and it gave United a giant first step toward the standard of personal customer service which was to make the name of the company synonymous with the "Friendly Skies.''

Early in his career Pat sensed the importance of the personnel aspects of the company. President Johnson, by necessity, concentrated on the many operating and technical ramifications of building an air system. Patterson saw that the people phase of the business was not neglected; selecting, training, and above all, motivating the men and women of the airline were recognized by him to be the essence of good management.

In those early days, Pat spoke out on his opinion that people were the company's most important capital:

"The balance sheet of United Airlines places no dollar and cents value on our employees but in my opinion they represent the most important asset our company has on its books. . . . When I think of employees, including management people, I think of how we in business treat an expensive machine, the high value we place on it, the care with which we use and maintain it or shift it to another part of the plant, and the preparations we make before we retire it from service. That machine shows up in the balance sheet at the end of every month, along with other assets, and there is a dollar value attached to it which we know we want to preserve. It is unfortunate that there isn't something on that balance sheet to indicate the value of employees we work with every day. If we could just put down something about 20,000 employees, value $80 million, maybe we'd be considerably more conscious of their value.''

Patterson spent endless hours and days and months becoming acquainted with the people of the Boeing air system. In time he knew each one by first name, and the employees knew him as "Pat." This was a great demonstration of his dedication to those associated with him, and for many years he was proud of his ability to know his fellow employees by their names. He knew more than their names; he knew their problems and he helped solve them; he knew their aptitudes and abilities and he encouraged them; he knew their aspirations and he helped them to progress, never in a paternal way, but always on a sincere personal plane.

In later years, Pat made this observation:

"I've always considered it a tribute, one that I cherish highly, that people on all levels of our business have called me by my first name. When I've gone through our shops and mechanics have said, 'Hello, Pat,' it has always made me feel good. The attitude of importance that comes over some men when they become top executives has always annoyed me. Too often the president's job is the loneliest and least secure in a company. . . .''

Out of this warm relationship grew United's outstanding reputation in the field of enlightened personnel policies, including such industry innovations as group insurance, pension planning, company medical services, wage and salary programs, and other important benefits.

Patterson's moves to motivate his organization were effectively cemented by his decision to continue full-scale operations when the airmail contracts were cancelled. From that point forward, Patterson's personal leadership of the company was a *fait accompli,* and he made the Rule of Five a living concept for all.

Chapter 6

A time of innovation

One of **Patterson's** fundamental traits was a lively curiosity. He took a keen interest in everything about the airline business—he wanted to know the why and how of things. His restless mind was alert to new ideas and to improvement in old ones. He was a dynamic manager, and he had no patience for the status quo; he believed in change, particularly in the airline business where change was vital to its development.

He sought out new ideas, testing them to see if they were good and dropping or adopting them as indicated. He encouraged his managers to try new approaches and methods; and when he felt lack of response, he sought ideas directly from employees. He installed the industry's first suggestion system, and over the years paid out hundreds of thousands of dollars for thousands of new ideas which led to improvements in the company's way of doing business. He opened up direct communications with employees in an open column published in the company's publication. Despite grumbling from some associates who felt their authorities were being bypassed, Patterson received and answered employee questions, some of which led to change and improvement. He wanted and got new ideas on many subjects: personnel practices, advertising and sales, accounting and the like. But in the earlier days he especially sought improvements in the company's operations, particularly in operational and in service areas.

During the mid-thirties after some extended traveling, Patterson literally got fed up with the fried chicken which dominated United and other airline menus. After looking unsuccessfully within the company for better food ideas, he sought the counsel of a food service consultant, Don Magarrell, later to become a United officer, who came up with the recommendation that United establish its own kitchen rather than buy the standard chicken dinners from airport restaurants and similar sources. Thus the company could control the quality and improve the variety of its in-flight menus. Like the stewardess idea, here was another service innovation which promised improvement. Almost overnight the idea was proved successful, and before long United was operating its own chain of flight kitchens at all its major air terminals, the first such company-operated food service in air transportation. The continental chefs supervising the kitchens took pride in seeing that United's passengers enjoyed the finest food aloft, and although the quality was the best, the kitchens proved to be more economical for the company as well. This innovation of Patterson's proved to be an advantage for the company in the competitive years to come.

Even more necessary were the technological improvements Patterson stimulated. No technical person himself, he knew how to find the right advisors, the most remarkable of whom was Thorp Hiscock, a Yakima hop rancher with a remarkably inventive mind and a deep interest in ham radio. Hiscock was William Boeing's brother-in-law, and one day when Boeing told Hiscock of the urgent need for two-way voice radio communication between planes and the ground—a system the leading companies in the field of radio said was impossible to develop—Hiscock volunteered to invent such a system, which he proceeded to do. Having produced a prototype of a workable voice radio system, Hiscock turned the plans over to Western Electric with a contract to build and install the system on United. This was to become the standard for all air transportation.

Hiscock was an innovator after Patterson's own style, and Pat equipped Thorp with not only a research laboratory in the company's Chicago hangars, but also with a full-time airplane for research and testing. In this Boeing 247 flying laboratory, a number of important devices were developed in United's quest for safety, the cardinal point in the company's Rule of Five.

One such device was an aircraft de-icer, critical but consistently elusive. One day Hiscock noticed a frozen flag dangling from the top of a pole and shedding flakes of ice whenever a breeze caused it to flap. He converted that observation into the concept of a thin rubber boot affixed to the leading edge of an aircraft wing, and alternately inflated and deflated by air pressure, thus cracking off any ice which might accumulate during flight. Goodyear applied this idea to the first successful aircraft de-icer which was standard in the industry until supplanted by the electrical heat system.

Similarly, out of United's ground and flight laboratories came the key to the first automatic pilot; a flight analyzer that was the prototype for today's flight recorder which automatically keeps a log of each airliner's flight path; a terrain indicator which paved the way for the modern radio altimeter; a device to eliminate static interference with radio communications on fast metal transports; the initial airport instrument landing system; and other major safety developments. With his emphasis upon improving operating safety, Patterson saw to it that United led the industry in this field for many years. And when the carriers, the manufacturers, and the government recognized that safety improvements should be developed on a total industry basis, he was satisfied to ground his flying laboratory and pool his efforts with others.

Patterson decided that the airline should take the lead in the development of new airliners, so he directed Jack Herlihy, United's engineering officer who was an M.I.T.

engineering graduate as well as a naval aviator, to determine what general characteristics were required for maximum safety, speed, and economy. In early 1936, Herlihy recommended a four-engined airplane carrying 40 passengers (twice the then current DC-3 size) and capable of maintaining flight on any two of its engines. Patterson then got United Aircraft, along with outside technical consultants, to help lay out design and specifications. With these blueprints Pat went to Seattle to test Boeing's interest in such a project, but Boeing was too busy developing a four-engine Clipper for Pan American to become involved. So he went to Santa Monica and found that Donald Douglas was indeed interested. With some cost estimates at hand, Patterson persuaded TWA, American, Eastern, and Pan American to join United, and a contract was negotiated between Douglas and the carriers for the prototype— Douglas to pay half the cost, the five carriers the other half.

This project was indeed an innovation, for it was unique in those days that several carriers would agree jointly to the design of a new airliner. In fact, it is still unique.

The prototype DC-4 was successfully flown in 1939. Douglas opened a DC-4 production line and United ordered 20 units. Long before deliveries could be started, the developing military crisis caused the War Department to request Patterson to waive United's contract so the DC-4's could go to the air corps. Hundreds of these airliners did tremendous air logistics duty in World War II as the army's C-54's and the navy's R-5D's. Not until 1946 did the DC-4 see commercial service, when United acquired 25 army surplus planes and operated them until Douglas could build and deliver a larger, faster, pressurized aircraft in 1947, the famous DC-6.

Patterson's far-sightedness in initiating the four-engine airliner concept not only served the national defense so effectively, but it started the whole new era of four-engined airliners capable of transcontinental flying and transoceanic as well, ending reliance on flying boats for overwater routes.

In the postwar period when nonscheduled operators were putting coach configurations into war surplus planes and operating "charter" flights on transcontinental schedules, few people remembered another United innovation of the Patterson era: the nation's first air coach service, initiated in twin-engine Lockheed airliners on the Los Angeles-San Francisco route in April, 1940.

Patterson had long believed the airline could profitably follow the example of railroads in providing both first-class and coach service. To differentiate the two, he felt they should be operated in separate aircraft; railroads had first-class and coach cars, and the airlines therefore should have first-class planes and then coach planes with the higher density seating. So a year and a half before World War II, United started its experimental coach service. But as the air corps began to require commercial airplanes for military use, the service had to be discontinued. In the postwar debate over nonskeds, and over how scheduled carriers should operate coach service, United temporarily appeared to be dragging its feet (when actually its concern was based mainly on safety factors involved in the density and type of seating). Patterson never was really credited with the coach concept he initiated in 1940.

Another of the many firsts credited to United was in air cargo when United converted DC-3's into "flying boxcars" and initiated New York-Chicago freight service in early 1941.

Air transport had gotten its start from airmail, but following Postmaster Brown's action in pushing the airlines into the passenger business, cargo had gradually taken a back seat and was no longer considered a front-line part of scheduled flying. Passenger traffic monopolized the airlines' attention, and mail, express, and freight were moving into the second cousin category.

Patterson had held to a conservative view of the future of air freight, while superoptimists were predicting air would take the freight away from rails and highways. He cautioned that as long as the airplane had to lift instead of pull, it would be no economic cargo match for the railroad, which simply added one freight car after another as cargo loads increased.

But he was aware that cargo did account for a significant share of United's revenues, and he had the vision to see that someday, somehow, somebody would develop air cargo into a profitable and important business. He intended that that somebody be United. United's entry into all-cargo operation as early as 1941, and its aggressive development of cargo market, would pave the way to the company's ultimate leadership in the U.S. scheduled airlines' air cargo market.

The list of Patterson innovations is long, and some were unsuccessful.

A notable failure among Patterson's ideas was the concept of one-class service. During the industry's first two decades, there was only one standard of service, at one fare. Then in the postwar period there was the spread of coach and economy services, along with a bewildering array of discount fares, cut rates, seasonal changes, volume reductions and other tariff debasements. The result was confusion personified among customers, travel agents, and airline personnel.

To straighten all this out, Pat conceived the strategy of restoring a single-class service. It would offer a five-abreast configuration throughout the airplane, and it would be priced well below first-class fares and somewhat higher than coach. Some of his associates believed the idea had good potential. Travel agents and traffic managers cheered the concept.

In 1963 United introduced its one-class service, and later in the year expanded it. The following year it was dropped. It had failed mainly because United's competitors cut their first-class fares to within a small amount of one-class, and added family plan rates to coach, which effectively sabotaged the one-class program. The CAB approved the competitive fare cut over United's protests. The one-class experiment was not only opposed by United's competitors, but by every other airline in the U.S., and in fact, the world. Air travelers were accustomed to the standard two-class pattern of service, and no single carrier—not even one as large as United—could prevail against the entire industry.

In retrospect, Pat believes United should have stood by its guns and fought a fare battle by further cutting its one-class fares and forcing the competitors and the CAB's hands, and that in the end one-class might have prevailed. He remained convinced that some day the whole industry would come to a single standard of service. He could well be proven right, but such a day lies far off in the future.

One-class service wasn't the only casualty among Patterson's innovations, it just happened to be the most spectacular. His conservatism often kept United from jumping in when competitors tried new ideas. United was among the last to serve liquor aloft, to show movies on long flights, and to operate club rooms for V.I.P.'s.

But over the years United did pace the industry in significant, progressive innovations, thanks in large part to Pat Patterson. And this had much to do with the company's world leadership.

Chapter 7

United goes to war

T
he first step United took in preparing for World War II, in concert with the other air carriers, was of far-reaching significance. As it turned out, the move was to insure air transport's commercial freedom in the postwar period, as opposed to the possibility of nationalization.

During 1941 word was received that President Roosevelt planned to take over the airlines upon the U.S. entry into the war, and to operate them as a branch of the government. Patterson and the other carrier presidents met to consider the problem, knowing that the results of such action could be catastrophic. They might never be able to disassemble a federal air system at war's end, and air transport could conceivably remain under permanent government control, as it was and still is in many countries. So Patterson and his contemporaries developed a plan of pooling their planes, their flight and ground personnel, and all their facilities to offer the army a ready-made airline system able to start military operations immediately.

When war did come in December, President Roosevelt prepared an executive order placing the airlines under General H. H. "Hap" Arnold commanding the army air force, but General Arnold himself argued successfully for the airlines' plan, which would give the air force what it needed without the long delay that would be necessary to reorganize the air system. Thus the plan prepared by

Patterson and the other carrier executives may well have avoided the nationalization of the industry in the postwar years.

Then, as in later years, Patterson was a strong believer in private enterprise, on which subject he has this to say:

"Our system of competitive enterprise offers ample latitude for achievement. You who inherit this system are its trustees. It will be in your custody to improve or impair. It's a wonderfully productive mechanism and it provides the world's highest standard of living. Granted there are imperfections but they are small in relation to total benefits. We must not be blind to social problems— to grievous defects in housing, health and education. Each of us has an obligation to take part in good works. The man who follows his own narrow way, heedless of misfortune around him, supplies government with reasons to go beyond its proper area. That area was defined many years ago by a man of great compassion, Abraham Lincoln. He said that government's proper role is to do for people what needs to be done that they cannot of themselves do at all or do so well."

United moved to separate its new military role from its continuing commercial mission by forming United Airlines Victory Corporation, a wholly-owned subsidiary, to operate air transport services for the government. Patterson specified this would be a nonprofit corporation, and United's first military contracts were on the basis of cost plus $1.00. Later, when the government decided United's services should be on the same basis as other air carriers, these contracts were revised to provide for a reasonable profit. (At the end of the war Patterson had an accounting made and determined there had been an excess profit of $296,000, a check for which he sent the government. A subsequent federal audit of United Victory Corporation's books confirmed that amount.)

United performed three fundamental roles in its military operations: the training of flight and ground crews, the modification of military aircraft, and the operation of air transport services.

Since 1929, Boeing Air Transport, and subsequently United Airlines, had been operating the Boeing School of Aeronautics at Oakland to train pilots and ground personnel for its air operations, and it had graduated several thousand personnel into the ranks of United and other airlines. In 1940, the U. S. Army Air Force contracted with the Boeing School to train military personnel, and later on the navy also turned to the school for training support. Before the close of the war, the Boeing school had trained 9,000 pilots, mechanics, navigators, meteorologists, and radio operators for military aviation, and the air force's technical training command gave the school a merit award for its valuable contribution.

The second mission in a way projected United into the airplane manufacturing business through modification of military planes, principally Boeing B-17 bombers. While the critically needed war planes were going through production, changes and additions of new accessories were constantly arising. These could not be performed at the factory without an unacceptable disruption of the production lines, so new airplanes were ferried to United's modification center (an expansion of its Cheyenne maintenance base) for the necessary rework before going into combat service. At peak, nearly 2,000 personnel manned the base, which by mid-1945 had modified 5,800 airplanes and turned out millions of B-17 spare parts. The modification center won an "A" rating for performance from the army air force, and the War Department recognized it with two "E" (for excellence) pennants.

The third military task was the most visible—conducting air transport operations. At war's outbreak, United had 69 DC-3 aircraft in its fleet—and 36 were drafted into military service under United's operational jurisdiction. (Half of the entire industry's fleet of 363 airliners went into military flying.)

United's first contract flying was a transcontinental

route from New York and San Francisco with supplementary schedules along the West Coast, and routes from supply centers at Dayton and Salt Lake City to our military bases in Alaska. For two years United maintained the Alaska services, during the early part of which Japanese attacks were experienced as the enemy carried out its combat operations against islands in the Aleutian chain. Despite the notoriously poor weather prevailing in this area and predictions of major difficulties, United's personnel for the Alaskan services operated five million airplane miles carrying 34,000 military passengers and thousands of tons of cargo without a single major accident. As an Alaska "bush" pilot remarked to a United captain: "You fellows have wiped out the myth about the dangers of flying in Alaska!"

United's most dramatic and extensive war service was in the Pacific theater. Beginning in September, 1942, and continuing until the end of 1946, United planes and pilots flew 200,000 passengers and 25,000 tons of cargo between California and the far reaches of the Pacific Rim. It was the largest airline operation in support of the great Pacific war.

The original Pacific route had Brisbane, Australia, as its terminus. As the campaigns of General Douglas MacArthur and Admiral Chester Nimitz moved northwestward toward Tokyo, so did United's forward base also move closely behind them—to New Guinea, to the Island of Biak, and to Guam.

Six weeks after its transpacific military contract was signed, United had trained 25 crews and a substantial ground force under the direction of veteran Seely Hall, and started up operations with a fleet of Convair-built four-engine "Liberators," later replaced by the C-54 version of the Douglas DC-4. Despite the company's lack of experience in long-range ocean flying, it established and maintained a noteworthy operating performance from the outset. Its unarmed planes were shot at by enemy fighter planes and plagued by Pacific storms.

Enemy bombing was so persistent at Canton Island that United's intermediate station was removed to Christmas Island. Enemy saboteurs were suspected of causing the crash of a "Liberator" aircraft which was United's only fatal accident during its far-flung Pacific flying.

In addition to regular schedules, United flew many special missions. One such trip took Captain Weldon "Dusty" Rhoades over 31,000 miles, from San Francisco via Washington to Brazil, Morocco, and Algiers, where he picked up Major General Richard Sutherland, chief of staff for General MacArthur, and flew him to Cairo to participate in the Big Three Conference held by Roosevelt, Churchill, and Chiang Kai-Shek. From Cairo Rhoades flew General Sutherland and his aides on back to the Pacific.

Sutherland was so impressed with Rhoades's airmanship that he requested Patterson to release him to become General MacArthur's personal pilot, which he did. Later on, before he retired as air force colonel to return to United, Rhoades flew MacArthur from Guam to Tokyo for his triumphant entry into the Japanese capital. All of United's Pacific planes and crews—along with many other Air Transport Command planes and pilots— carried the military men and materials to take over the conquered country, in a great airlift between Okinawa and Japan.

Meanwhile the balance of United's DC-3 fleet was working overtime to provide a minimum commercial service on its domestic routes. There was a great demand for available seats from both military and business travelers, so the Office of Defense Transportation established a priority system to govern the use of scheduled airline seats. Standby lists were long, and consequently the annual system load factor climbed from 66 percent in 1941 to an incredible 96 percent in 1944. After that year DC-3's were returned to United as hundreds of new Douglas C-54's took over the full mission of military supply.

Assessing the war's impact on United, there were some major effects:

The airline industry had demonstrated its great value to national defense and its capacity to perform without government takeover.

The industry had also proved it was indispensable in serving the nation's business and commerce at a time of their greatest need.

United had accumulated a great reserve of flight and ground experience with the four-engined DC-4, which it would use as the prime unit of its immediate postwar fleet.

The company had gained invaluable expertise in long-range Pacific flying, which would be an asset in its future bid to operate between California and Hawaii.

Not the least important benefit to the industry was the remarkable stimulation of peacetime air travel on the part of service people and civilians alike. There developed a deep pent-up demand that would furnish the airlines with a much bigger market at the close of the war—and yet provide some of the biggest headaches the carriers had ever experienced.

Chapter 8

The Patterson years

Postwar

V-J Day did not signal the end of United's engagement in the war. It would operate its transpacific military flights until the close of 1946.

However, during the summer of 1945, between the surrender of Germany and the collapse of Japan, Patterson and his associates turned their attention to postwar planning. Economists were forecasting a great postwar boom with the nation's transition from a wartime to a peace economy. Millions of servicemen would be returning to take up jobs in business and industry that would be taxed to supply the postwar demand for consumer goods and services. Certainly the airlines faced a rosy future, with a strong travel market growth expected as the peacetime economy geared up and millions of travelers took to the air. In this optimistic atmosphere, United began to implement its plan for expansion.

The forecasters proved to be right about the coming boom, but they failed to anticipate its suddenness and intensity. Overnight, the people of the United States wanted everything, and at once.

The expected prosperous growth of United (and other carriers) turned into a nightmare. Its too few planes were swamped with the rush of air travelers, its personnel were inadequate to handle the avalanche of business, airport terminals of prewar dimensions were overrun, airways were overcrowded, schedule dependability was bogged down, and "What's the matter with the airlines?" became a favorite topic at cocktail parties.

To make matters worse, on October 15, 1945, the War Department abolished its wartime system of passenger priorities for travel. It was a premature move, for the nation was still wrestling with the mammoth job of returning military personnel to their homes. The end of the priority system brought hordes of civilian travelers to the airline counters, competing with homeward-bound GI's for space on the airlines' still depleted fleets. The outcome was a shambles, and at United's request to protect the returning servicemen, the War Department issued a new order reserving for military personnel 70 percent of passenger space on commercial flights eastbound from the Pacific Coast. That order remained in effect until February, 1946.

Then with the last of the wartime restrictions on air travel abolished, civilians resumed their rush to the airline counters.

The airlines were unable to cope with the flood of demand. There were too few planes, too few personnel, too few facilities. *Fortune* magazine summed up the problem in its August, 1946, issue:

"The cause of the trouble is simple enough: boom business. The boom is enormous by any comparison, and it came with unexpected suddenness and intensity. This boom came to a business that was handicapped by almost completely obsolete ground facilities and was deeply understaffed.

"Few airline executives foresaw the extent of the present boom; none came near guessing correctly the depth of the packed-down public demand for air travel. Rates have been reduced 10 per cent since 1941, making it cheaper in many cases to travel by air than by Pullman —bringing in even greater hordes of travel-bargain customers."[1]

1. "What's Wrong with the Airlines," *Fortune* (August, 1946).

While *Fortune* may have been correct about airline executives having underestimated the dimensions of the postwar boom, there was little they could have done about it in advance.

Once the problem surfaced, Patterson acted quickly. "I am greatly disturbed about the breakdown of our efficiency," he said. "This very serious problem requires the attention of United's first team of management."

His first move was to appoint a group of senior officers to go out into the field, visit the key stations, and take action on local managers' recommendations for correcting problems and improving service where possible without delay. Dubbed "The Atomic Committee," the top management team worked with managers in the field to solve many day-to-day operating problems and to bring some improvement in current service to the public.

But the real answers would take time, for the major problems were fundamentally long term.

Patterson laid out five basic planning areas: planes, personnel, routes, finances, and marketing.

Planes:

United had gone into the war with 69 DC-3's, and with the return of those and the addition of more from air force surplus (DC-4's were doing the full military mission before war's end), it had 77 DC-3's in its 1945 fleet. Patterson then purchased 25 surplus army DC-4's for interim expansion, and with that temporary solution to the capacity problem, turned his attention to longer-range fleet planning.

One of the bright linings of the black clouds of war is the fact that civil aviation always benefits from the great acceleration of aircraft technology when cost becomes secondary to need. Significant developments for military aircraft are subsequently applied to commercial airliners —in better aircraft design and construction, better engines, and better navigation and communication devices.

Thus, the DC-4—Patterson's "dream" airliner of the late thirties and the long-haul "workhorse" of the military services—was obsolete before the conclusion of the war. Douglas had applied many improvements to the design of a new type transport designated the DC-6—a larger, faster, more efficient version of the DC-4, including cabin pressurization among other refinements. This meant the DC-6 could be flown at much higher altitudes than its unpressurized predecessors, going high into the smooth upper levels above most storms, and enabling schedules to be operated more comfortably and more dependably. United ordered 35 DC-6's, and in the end had a total of 89 DC-6 and DC-6B units in its fleet. The first DC-6 went into transcontinental service in April, 1947, and before it was finally retired, it proved to be the best four-engine propeller plane ever built.

Along with the DC-6, United needed a smaller type to replace its short-haul DC-3's. It selected the Martin designed 303, a 40-passenger twin-engine pressurized plane that on paper best suited the company's small-plane requirements. As far as United was concerned, the 303 remained a paper plane, for costs and construction delays forced cancellation of the 303 contract. Ultimately the company went to Convair for a fleet of 55 Convair 340 twin-engined short-range planes which admirably filled its requirements in this area through the piston era.

Two other propeller types were involved in the postwar period. Both were popular with travelers but headaches for United: they were the DC-7 and the Boeing Stratocruiser.

While the DC-6 was a great airplane, it lacked transcontinental nonstop range. Mainly at the instigation of American Airlines, Douglas developed the DC-7, about the same size as the DC-6B, but equipped with new Curtiss-Wright turbocompound piston engines which, with greater fuel capacity, powered the DC-7 from coast to coast with plenty of reserve and somewhat more speed. Unfortunately the costs were considerably higher than for the DC-6, and the new engines were notoriously undependable. Furthermore, the prospect of jet-powered airliners was developing rapidly. Nevertheless, airline competition being as intense as it was—and is—United ordered 25 DC-7's, knowing their useful lives would be short and their operational problems severe.

Boeing had developed a huge (for that time) plane as its entry in the postwar airliner sweepstakes to compete with Douglas's DC-6 and Lockheed's Constellation. This was the 377, better known as the Stratocruiser, with a passenger capacity of 80 passengers, including aft staterooms, and a large lower deck lounge. The Stratocruiser seemed ideal for United's new California-Hawaii route. The company ordered seven units for 1947 delivery. It received its first two years late; and while the roomy, quiet plane was immensely popular with passengers, it was costly to operate and full of "bugs" mainly associated with its large, new engines. After a few years of red-ink operation, the company sold the Stratocruisers to a foreign carrier and used DC-7's for the Hawaiian service until the advent of the jets.

Personnel:

As war ended, the 1,500 United men and women who took leaves of absence to join the services returned to their company, and the hundreds of flight crews and ground personnel who manned the company's military operations were phased back into their regular jobs, so that 8,000 total employees represented the company's payroll by the summer peak of 1946. Before the end of that year the number of employees was *doubled* in a frantic drive to meet the onslaught of postwar passengers. But even a one-million-dollar crash training program could not help qualify eager but inexperienced employees to solve the company's passenger-handling problems overnight.

By 1947 the bloom was off the postwar traffic boom. In addition, the acquisition of planes and the expansion of ground facilities had pushed up United's costs, so that by 1948 it was necessary to retrench, and a cutback of 4,000 employees—25 percent of the total payroll—was undertaken. Even with the best planning, United discovered that unforeseen events like the flattening of the air travel market could upset the airline applecart and cause change of direction and curtailment.

At the same time, Patterson learned that his long-time practice of personal contact with employees would no longer work on a person-to-person basis, for the company had grown too large for him to be able to know each employee. In the fall of 1945, Pat loaded some of his fellow officers into a DC-3 to cover all of United's stations and to meet with as many people at each station as possible. In 32 days they had covered 36 stations, his associates were on the ropes, and Pat was in a San Francisco hospital being treated for exhaustion.

This experience dictated new approaches—anniversary dinners for groups, written question-and-answer communication between employees and the president, and so on. More importantly, it focused his attention on employee benefit programs like the Credit Union, the Mainliner and Management Clubs, and other methods of personnel motivation.

Patterson also studied the company's postwar organization structure. In the formative days it had functioned with four operating divisions, then with three. During the war period the company was brought under centralized management to deal better with the rapidly shifting problems and the separate military services. The first postwar organizational move to establish two operating divisions, east and west, was shelved later for a different approach to decentralization. The purely operational functions of flight, passenger service, and ground operations were relocated to Denver at the geographical center of the airline; engineering and maintenance remained at its San Francisco base at the directional hub of the system (from whence planes went north, east, south, and west, making overhaul work most convenient), and the corporate functions of finance, marketing, planning, law, and medicine stayed at the Chicago general offices. But as the Jet Age approached, Pat felt it was time to centralize once more, and with the construction of its present Chicago executive office building, United's corporate and operating activities were again joined under one roof.

Routes:

United entered the postwar years with its same route pattern—from coast to coast and along the Pacific seaboard. During the war the company had received a number of awards to new cities with start of service to await peace: Boston, Hartford, Washington, D.C., Detroit, some smaller California cities, Milwaukee, some points in Oregon. Service to all such points was completed by 1947; this added further to the complications of the postwar stretch, but also materially strengthened United's system.

Patterson and his colleagues looked ahead and saw still further additions which were considered essential.

One was a direct transcontinental entry to Los Angeles, which United served only on its route via San Francisco. In 1938 United had planned to purchase Western Air Express which operated between Los Angeles and Salt Lake City, but though Western's stockholders approved the merger as did the CAB's examiner, Western's president and a minority stockholder group succeeded in having the CAB members deny it. Patterson then filed for a new route from Denver to Los Angeles, but Western applied for the route and got it. Next United filed for a route from Omaha to Los Angeles, but by that time Western Airlines ran into financial problems that threatened bankruptcy, and in 1947 sold its Denver-Los Angeles certificate to United for $3,750,000, including four DC-4's. This finally gave United direct transcontinental access to Los Angeles.

Another market Patterson wanted was Hawaii. There was nothing personal about this; he and his management were convinced Hawaii would become one of the world's premier tourist markets.

Prior to the war the San Francisco-Honolulu route was

operated exclusively by Pan American. United applied for two routes to Hawaii—one originating from San Francisco, the other from Los Angeles. In its application, the company cited its experience flying the transpacific route for the Air Transport Command during the war and expressed its optimism over the future of Hawaii as a commercial and tourist center. The CAB was equally optimistic, and on May 17, 1946, awarded United the San Francisco-Honolulu route, while denying the Los Angeles-Honolulu segment. Service on the new route was launched May 1, 1947.

In 1950 United was also granted rights to operate between Los Angeles and Honolulu. Ten years later, it had built its Hawaiian service to such a point that it carried 60 percent of air passengers between California and the Islands, and the Waipahu-born Patterson had seen his prediction of a major Hawaiian tourist market come true, thanks in large part to United's planes and their promotion.

Still another question facing United was that of international routes, particularly transpacific to the Far East.

Patterson had taken his company through one abortive international expedition during the war. The Mexican Government had invited Patterson to look at an airline named LAMSA (Lineas Aereas Mineras, S.A.). As its Spanish name suggests, it was an airline started originally to supply remote interior mines and to fly out their minerals. Now its 1,700 miles of airway were going no place, and Mexico felt it needed both capital and counsel to succeed. Patterson offered both, and with the approval of the CAB and the Mexican Government, supplied money (ultimately in the amount of $5 million) and a management team. The health of LAMSA within Mexico began to improve, but United got absolutely no place with its objective of hooking LAMSA up with United at, say, Los Angeles and providing a unified route between Vancouver, B.C. and Seattle on the one hand, and Mexican points on the other. Finally, when it became apparent United would be thwarted in this strategy and LAMSA would continue to drain United's dollars, Patterson unloaded the airline to a group of Mexican financiers. (Western ultimately got the Los Angeles-Mexico City route, and it has been a good one.) This experience did not precondition him to view with much enthusiasm the prospect of an international route.

Most U.S. carriers were hot after postwar overwater routes. Because of its major military contract across the Pacific including its participation in the occupation of Japan, many executives at United urged the company to go after a transocean certificate to the Orient. Patterson had his economists study the international markets, and their reports indicated that based on prewar data and assuming the bilateral presence of many foreign flag carriers both on the Pacific and Atlantic, traffic would be uneconomically thin, at least for the initial five years of any operation. Based upon this and more importantly on his conviction that the nation's future "Merchant Marine of the Air" would be best served if the country would support a single strong carrier against the many foreign airlines certain to be spawned, Patterson expressed support when Juan Trippe of Pan American advanced his "chosen instrument" concept.

The concept was essentially to be a cartel: Pan American to be the single U.S. international operator, in which each domestic U.S. airline might have an investment, share in connecting traffic and in earnings. The chosen instrument would be one big and strong airline that could compete effectively with numerous foreign government-owned lines. All the other domestic carriers opposed the notion, and the CAB disapproved it. Not too long afterwards, United won its Hawaii routes and chewed up Pan American in competing for this traffic, proving that, as someone has observed, airline politics makes changing bedfellows.

From time to time the CAB acted on postwar applications to expand the domestic route structure. None of

71

the Board's actions (until the Transpacific Case which came later) had the broad effect involved in the Board's 1955 route case largesse when it added American to the New York-Chicago-San Francisco airway; put United into Kansas City and TWA into Denver; added United and American to TWA's Pittsburgh stronghold; and with many other lesser awards thoroughly congested the airline map, although pointing out it gave no route award that was not applied for by some airline.

Finances:

As early as 1942, United's management had set aside $2.5 million reserves for postwar readjustment, and during the war years the company followed a policy of cash conservation. From December 31, 1941, to the end of 1945, earned surplus had increased from $152,000 to $11.8 million which, together with $1.5 million of capital surplus, provided United with a good equity base for its planned $85 million postwar expansion through 1948.

During the years after the war, additional financing was frequently necessary to support the rapid flight and ground equipment expansion. In addition, during 1951 United and the other members of the so-called "Big Four" airlines went off the airmail subsidies which had supported the early development of the commercial air network (a form of support in principle not unlike the government's land grants to the pioneering railroads).

More and more it was to insurance companies and banks that United and other airlines turned for financing, setting a pattern that would characterize the very substantial loans that would be required later to launch and extend the Jet Age. Curtis Barkes, originally in the National Air Transport organization, emerged as United's chief financial officer through the latter days of the postwar period, planning the huge financing program which would support the first and second generation jets.

Patterson often spoke out on the need for a profitable airline industry:

"In our country—the world's prime example of economic progress—there are those who regard profits with hostility. They seem to believe that normal healthy returns are rather sinful and that large returns are downright immoral. In their lexicon, as someone has said, profit is a dirty word. My question is, would we have a better air transportation system if there were no profits? Would it be better if the airlines made just a little profit, enough to keep them alive but feeble? Or is the industry entitled to a healthy profit that will permit it to pay good wages and ample dividends, to liquidate debts expeditiously and accumulate financial strength for further advances?"

Marketing:

Air transportation's first 50 years represent one of the great success stories of modern marketing and merchandising. In that period the airlines started from scratch in the long-haul passenger business and wound up displacing the railroads so completely that many of them virtually dropped out of the passenger business.

There had to be and there was a tremendous improvement in safety and quality of air service to make it sufficiently appealing to the public to counteract the basic fear of flying. Speed tripled from 100 miles per hour to 300 miles per hour and was to reach twice that with the subsonic jets of the sixties.

Dependability was improved commensurately, with schedule regularity becoming the rule in the "Flying Fifties." In-flight comfort and service were enhanced too. Pressurized cabins, attractive course meals, and steadily lowering fares had much to do with gaining customers. The biggest factor was great improvement in safety.

But the service had to be sold, and it was sold effectively. During all its prewar and some of its postwar years, United's top salesman was Vice-President Harold Crary, organizer of the Air Transport Association in the latter twenties. During the postwar years, he was succeeded by Robert E. Johnson, who directed United's traffic development from sales to the modern marketing concept.

Chapter 9

Capital merger

Over the years Patterson had repeatedly said his objective was to run not the biggest, but the best airline. During the prewar years, United was second in size, outranked by American. In 1961, however, United did become the largest airline in the Free World, and as a result, for a brief period it was certainly far from being the best one.

The occasion was the acquisition of Capital Airlines, and putting the nation's fifth largest airline together with United not only propelled the company into first place among all airlines excepting Russia's monopolistic Aeroflot, but it produced a massive headache caused by the difficult problems of assimilation.

The Capital deal was the largest airline merger to occur, and it was the last trunk carrier action of its kind until Delta acquired Northeast in 1972. In both cases imminent financial failure led to CAB approval of the takeovers. None of the many other merger proposals during the intervening years involved this factor, and all were denied.

Merger was nothing new to United. It had sprung from the union of four carriers, and in the succeeding years it acquired several other carriers or parts of them: Stout Air Services, West Coast Air Transport, Wyoming Air Service's Cheyenne-Denver Division, and the Denver-Los Angeles run of Western Airline. Nor was merger anything new to Capital: it counted five airlines in the branches of its family tree.

During the formative prewar years Capital had grown to a substantial and profitable operation serving 23 cities in the populous triangle from Chicago and Detroit through Cleveland and Pittsburgh to Washington and Baltimore and to the southeast. By the end of the war the company had plans to expand not only across the U.S., but over the Atlantic and Pacific as well to Europe, Africa, Alaska, and South America. At first its ambitious route applications bore little fruit. All it received in new routes was one between Pittsburgh and New York, and operating rights to compete with United, TWA, American, and Northwest between New York and Chicago. Capital acquired war surplus DC-4's to cover its postwar service, and ordered new DC-6's to become competitive with the larger carriers.

But profits failed to follow expansion, and Capital met the first of a series of financial crises that would lead to its takeover by United. The DC-6 order was cancelled, and J. H. "Slim" Carmichael, an aviator who had risen to the executive vice-presidency of the company, became president and chief executive officer. He instituted economies that included dropping one-third of Capital's employees and management officials. From a net loss of $2.6 million in 1946, Capital showed a $2.7 million profit in 1947. With this turnaround accomplished, Carmichael turned to future expansion.

During the next few years, Capital gained franchises to Minneapolis, Philadelphia, Atlanta, and New Orleans, among other points, and succeeded in freeing itself from restrictions against longer-range nonstop services between its key terminals, thus projecting itself into more head-to-head competition with the "Big Four" carriers. This focused attention upon Capital's weakness: equipment. Its fleet of DC-4's could not compete with DC-6's and Constellations, so Carmichael decided to purchase some Constellations, which helped to offset its airplane disadvantage in the marketplace.

The string of profitable years lengthened under Carmichael's leadership, but by 1950 it became evident that the capital investment required to keep the company moving profitably up its planned growth curve would be out of reach. So in 1952 the board of directors concluded merger was the only logical answer. That year, after an abortive attempt to negotiate with Northwest Airlines, Capital turned to United. Some preliminary discussions were held, but a stumbling block was the condition that Charles Murchison, then Capital's largest stockholder who served as the company's general counsel and executive committee chairman, would serve in the same capacities with United. This was unacceptable to Patterson and the negotiations were dropped.

Meanwhile, the total air market was growing steadily. Capital had relied upon marketing and service strategies to try to gain its share of that growth. It created the innovation of night coach fares, one-third lower than regular air rates, with a "no-frills" service on flights operating at late-night hours. This was so successful it became a permanent feature of airline tariffs. Also Capital's marketers were among the first to see the potential in charter traffic, and as early as 1943, Capital was the industry's leading charter operator.

With no merger prospects in sight, the Capital management decided its future welfare depended upon route expansion and new equipment, and it elected to work in both of those directions. Instead of attaining future prosperity, the result would be disastrous.

In the equipment field, Capital was already competing against the new DC-7's; the turboprop Electra was about to make its debut, and the first straight jets were not far off. Capital needed a major fleet modernization program, although the relatively short-haul characteristics of its route system did not require the range of the DC-7, for example.

In June, 1954, Carmichael returned from London where he had spent some time reviewing British aircraft, and announced that the airline was placing an order for three Viscount turboprop aircraft manufactured by Vickers-Armstrongs, Ltd. of England, and was taking an option on an additional 37 Viscounts. The 40-plane package carried a price tag of $45 million, and the British offered a tempting installment plan for their purchase.

Two months later Capital exercised its option on the 37 Viscounts and took new options on 20 more of the British turboprops. These latter options were exercised on December 2, 1954, bringing the carrier's new aircraft commitments to a 60-airplane, $70.3 million package, on which Capital made a modest down payment of $3.6 million and signed notes with Vickers and Rolls Royce, Ltd., the engine manufacturer, for the balance of $66.7 million.

Delivery of the new airplanes began in 1955, and when the Viscounts were introduced on the Chicago-Washington, D.C. route in July of that year, the aircraft immediately found favor with passengers.

The 48-seat cabin configuration, 350-mph speed that was equalled only by the brand new DC-7's, and the smooth, quiet ride offered by the turboprop jetliners, represented a competitive edge that siphoned traffic from Capital's rivals. When Capital closed 1955 with $4.1 million in net profits, Carmichael was convinced his airline had no place to go but up.

At the same time the CAB had been cooperating by eliminating Capital's route restrictions on key segments and granting Capital major new routes into the Southeast and Southern United States. Now Carmichael and his associates had their long-sought opportunity to compete with the top trunks on an even, nonstop basis across such prime routes as New York-to-Chicago and Washington-to-Chicago. And these marketing opportunities turned Carmichael's attention to pure jets. The Douglas DC-8 and the Boeing 707 were too big and too long in range to fit Capital's requirements, so Carmichael went to England again, this time ordering 14 turbojet Comets.

They would never be delivered.

From 1955's profit, Capital slipped into the red in 1956, and by 1957 it was apparent it would not be able to meet the installment payment schedule on its Viscount fleet.

As the crisis worsened, Major General Davis Baker, retired from the air force, was brought in to replace Carmichael in 1957. George Hann, Pittsburgh founder of a predecessor airline, became chairman of the executive committee. Baker and Hann promptly cancelled the Comet order and proceeded to order 15 Convair 880 jets, the smaller jet airliner developed by General Dynamics. These wouldn't be delivered either.

Even at this late hour, Capital and the CAB failed to recognize that giving more new routes to Capital was no panacea, but actually worsened the problem by overstretching the company's resources. When the Board awarded more routes from the north into Miami, Tampa, and other Florida points, the airline found itself sinking in a sea of new routes and unpaid-for planes.

Of its original $66 million obligation on the Viscount fleet, only $35 million had been repaid to Vickers. By the end of 1959, $10 million of the loan was overdue, and $14 million more would be due on January 1, 1960. Attempts to negotiate refinancing of Capital's total debt structure were unsuccessful. The carrier also failed in its attempts to obtain federal subsidy from the CAB.

Since early 1958, Vickers had accommodated Capital on its requests for deferral of payments while the airline explored a new financing program. However, first quarter losses of $5.5 million in 1960 and indications of further losses in the second quarter killed the carrier's chances for refinancing; and in April 1960, Vickers instituted formal foreclosure proceedings in the U.S. Court for the Southern District of New York.

Capital's board of directors turned to Thomas D. Neelands, Jr., a Capital director since 1948 and chairman of its finance committee from early 1956 until his resignation from the board in 1958. Neelands was elected chairman of the board, having accepted the position on the sole condition that he would have a free hand in negotiating a merger transaction, the only solution that he saw for the beleaguered airline.

Neelands got Vickers to delay its foreclosure action. Merger possibilities were immediately explored, but Neelands had one turndown after another. Eastern and American had expressed disinterest in absorbing Capital. Northwest was ruled out, for it did not then have the financial strength to present an attractive offer to Vickers. Neelands also considered a three-way merger involving Capital, Northwest and Delta, but Delta was not interested.

Neelands then dispatched an emissary to United's Patterson. Although he had been on the Capital board when Patterson rejected the 1952 merger proposal, Neelands believed United had the capacity to absorb Capital, and would benefit from its acquisition.

Patterson became convinced that a merger with United was the only move that could save Capital from bankruptcy. On the other hand, he refused to negotiate in the spirit that United had Capital's back to the wall. He was considering the possible benefits of merger to United and to Capital's employees, shareholders, and customers.

Although Capital had been unable to realize reasonable profits from its routes over an extended period of time; although its Viscounts represented a new breed of aircraft that were not fully competitive with the newer jetliners and therefore had no place in United's overall equipment program; and although there would be inevitable problems and expenses incident to a merger, Patterson also saw the positive aspects of a takeover.

A merger with Capital would remove a serious threat to the credit of the entire airline industry; would eliminate restrictions on United which the CAB had imposed to protect Capital; would provide relief from the seasonal traffic imbalance that plagued United; would eliminate unneeded competition on routes United served with Capital; would generate additional revenues and provide some tax-loss carry-over.

Patterson asked Curtis Barkes, United's senior financial officer, to work out merger details with Capital, and the discussions culminated with the two carriers and Vickers filing a letter of merger intent on July 19, 1960. Within a month, the directors and stockholders of both airlines approved the merger proposal, and on August 11, 1960, the parties applied to the CAB for approval of the merger.

The merger conditions were attractive enough to Capital's stockholders and to Vickers's. Each share of Capital common stock was to be exchanged for one-seventh of a share of United common, plus a stock purchase warrant entitling the holder to buy three-fourteenths of a share of United common at $40 per share during the next five years. Holders of Capital's 4-1/2 percent convertible subordinated debentures were offered 20 shares of United common for each $1,000 of debentures.

On its part, Vickers was to receive 159,000 shares of United's 5-1/2 percent $100-par-value preferred stock, 60,000 shares of United common stock, and stock purchase warrants to buy 200,000 shares of United common stock at $45 per share during the next 7-1/2 years. In addition, Vickers would take back 15 of the Viscounts in Capital's fleet.

The merger agreement was conditioned upon its approval by the CAB prior to February 1, 1961, and upon the absence of any terms and conditions which, in the judgment of United's directors, would have a substantially adverse effect upon United.

The CAB proceeding which followed was a landmark in administrative cases, not only for the speed with which the CAB dispatched the case, but also for the manner in which the CAB kept intact virtually all of the merger terms.

Actually, the CAB had no alternative, other than

bankruptcy for Capital. The latter course would have left Capital's 7,600 employees jobless in an already-saturated labor market, deprived Vickers and Capital stockholders of fair returns on their investments, and thrown airline service on Capital's routes into utter confusion.

On April 3, 1961, the CAB approved the United-Capital merger, imposing only two major conditions: (a) United's use of actual purchase price, rather than book value of Capital's assets, in establishing its investment base for the acquisition; and (b) imposition of labor protective provisions for the benefit of United and Capital employees.

Anticipating CAB approval of the merger, United meanwhile had formed a merger planning committee, composed of key employees from both companies, which developed policies and procedures to ensure a smooth changeover on merger date. Seniority rosters had to be integrated, employees relocated, job nomenclatures and wage bands standardized, and most important of all, schedules had to be consolidated.

On June 1, 1961, Capital Airlines, an enterprise that rose from a barnstorming operation to a position as the nation's fifth largest carrier, passed from the scene. It had fought a valiant struggle in the business world, and failed. With its passing, United emerged as the Free World's biggest airline, with 30,275 employees and 264 airplanes serving 118 cities in an 18,000-mile system.

United's Patterson was delighted, but hardly awestruck. Size, to him, was not the true test of an airline's greatness. It was quality: of operation, of service, of philosophy, of fundamental character. "I still want to run the world's best airline, not necessarily the biggest," he said.

For the next few months, Patterson was to preside over an operation that was far below his standards of quality. The dislocation caused by the integration of the Capital system into United was inevitable, and it was severe. Despite the careful planning of the merger committee, there were plenty of loose ends and rough edges only time could correct. But more importantly, the physical and personnel changes made necessary by the phasing in of the Capital operation were monumental, and had an adverse effect on United's entire operation. Until these changes could be made, until the former Capital personnel could adapt to United's way of doing things, schedules could be readjusted and service smoothed out, there was an acute case of corporate indigestion.

United's established customers were quick to complain about schedule delays and service lapses, while Capital's customers were equally quick to complain about the failure of overnight improvement of schedules and service in their areas. With respect to the latter, Patterson had anticipated that problem, and in fact well before the merger was approved, had leased Capital two Boeing 720 jets to operate in its strategic Great Lakes-Florida market. After the merger was in effect, he played a "watchdog" role in seeing that the former Capital Southeast territory received its share of new schedules.

In the post-merger months, the problems were gradually solved, schedule dependability was restored, and high standards of service reestablished. In the end, Patterson saw that United more than fulfilled its assurance that excepting for its officers, every Capital employee would become a United employee with fair and equal status. The words "former Capital" were systematically eliminated from United's vocabulary.

A decade later it appeared the merger had produced several major benefits:

It had prevented the airline industry from the damaging effects otherwise caused by a Capital bankruptcy, and in the process it preserved the welfare of the 7,600 Capital employees.

It added significant new markets to United's system. This was not an unmixed advantage, for some of the former Capital territory was infertile and resulted in red ink at the bottom line. On the other hand, the routes from Buffalo, Cleveland, and Pittsburgh to Florida, among others, and the additions of such prime markets as Atlanta and the Twin Cities have brought positive results.

Even more significant was the strengthening of United in markets it had previously shared with Capital but had been severely handicapped by route restrictions—Pittsburgh, Washington, Cleveland, Detroit, for example. Also important has been the cross-feed of traffic moving across parts of both United and Capital systems.

Finally, United did become the Free World's largest air carrier. There is penalty associated with bigness. People tend to look at bigness with suspicion and doubt, and are apt to construe incidents of substandard service as the product of bigness. Bigness can become a problem for management, and constant discipline is essential to avoid the inertia and indifference which can creep into a big organization. But there are positives in size, and they should and do outweigh the negatives.

Being the biggest offers the opportunity of leadership in its fullest sense. The biggest is not always the leader, but the biggest always has the opportunity to achieve leadership. It has been in the stewardship of this responsibility that United has striven to fulfill the challenge of the merger, and has built a heritage for future United generations.

Chapter 10

The first jet age

The Jet Age was born in World War II with the turbojet engines developed by the British and the Germans, and first applied to fighters by the Luftwaffe. In allocating air priorities, the U.S. had taken the big job of mass producing piston engines and propeller aircraft, while Great Britain put its emphasis upon developing jet power. By war's end it was a reality.

While plans to shift United back to a peacetime footing were moving ahead, Patterson was thinking of the future jet era already on the horizon. He knew that United would have to buy and launch a large piston-engined air fleet for its first postwar service, but planning would have to be initiated for its jet replacement. The brilliant engineer who had spearheaded the jet project for England, Sir Frank Whittle, had convinced Patterson that jet airliners would be a reality within a decade. Already Great Britain was at its aeronautical drawing boards to convert its military jet expertise to commercial advantage, and the British Comet was much more than a glint in an engineer's eye. Patterson summoned Jack Herlihy, his senior engineering officer.

"Let's start looking ahead to jets," Patterson said. "Keep up with what the British are doing, and figure out what United will need. Get a fix on how and when jets will affect us, and what we should do about them." His foresight had much to do with the fact that United would be the first domestic airline to order jet airliners.

Within five years Herlihy had given United a running start into the Jet Age. After several trips to England, Herlihy became convinced the Comet would not be a successful jet airliner; he felt it would be too small to achieve the economic benefits of jet power, and he was concerned that its construction would not be adequate to cope with the stringent environment of jet speeds and altitudes. His judgment was substantiated in 1953 when the production Comet, entering commercial service in Europe years ahead of U.S. jet transport planes, had to be grounded. Later, improved models would not be able to compete with the first of the larger U.S. jets appearing toward the end of the decade.

Herlihy thought he knew what United would need in a jet airliner—its size, its operating performance, and its economics. In 1952 he started United's first jet service— the "Paper Jet" airline. A special task group simulated round-trip schedules between San Francisco and New York, and between San Francisco and Chicago every day, putting the theoretical airplanes across the airways under the weather conditions actually existing, calculating how much fuel would be burned, at what altitudes optimum performance would be achieved, what kind of payloads would produce a profit against fully allocated costs, and a myriad of other operational tests. Gradually the paper jet airline yielded its data, and that data validated United's own aircraft specification requirements.

Two leading manufacturers were developing jet airliners—Boeing and Douglas. Except for the big Stratocruiser which it couldn't sell in sufficient quantity to make it successful, Boeing had concentrated its postwar attention on military aircraft which it had developed so brilliantly during the war with its famous B-17 and B-29 piston bombers. Now it built the long range B-52 jet bomber which became the mainstay of the nation's air defense system. The Strategic Air Command sought to extend the B-52's range by mid-air refueling, and so Boeing developed the KC 135, a fatter-bodied jet tanker, which the air force ordered in production quantity. Seeing in its tanker the potential for a commercial jet airliner, Boeing proceeded to develop the prototype for the 707. With a real life jet transport plane to demonstrate, Boeing went out to sign up airline customers.

Meanwhile Douglas had dominated the postwar world transport plane market with its highly successful DC-6, followed by the DC-7. Its engineers had been busy with jet development as well, and were translating its background of commercial experience into its concept of the ideal jet airliner, designated as the DC-8. There was no flying prototype—the best Douglas could do was to build a wooden mock-up to represent its size and cabin configuration.

United devoted a great deal of time to evaluating the two aircraft—both were good on paper, but Boeing had the advantage of an actual airplane. Then United discovered a difference. United wanted six-abreast seating in the coach compartment. Douglas could accommodate this configuration, but Boeing's prototype model was too narrow—by just four inches, but those inches made the difference. United asked Boeing to widen its fuselage, but it was intended that the 707 production line would use the same dies as the KC 135, and Boeing said it couldn't change them, and that its cabin would stay at five-abreast coach seating width.

In October, 1955, United placed the first domestic airline order for jet transport planes—$175 million worth of Douglas DC-8's—30 in all. It could have received the 707 at least six months earlier than the Douglas delivery date of mid-1959, but the jets would operate for a long time, and Patterson wanted the "wide" cabin. Surprised by the loss of United's contract and determined to capture other airline orders, Boeing then widened its cabin to meet Douglas's competition, and did very well selling its jet airliner. Both the Douglas DC-8 and the Boeing 707 turned out to be great aircraft. United's decision in favor of the DC-8 insured competition and that meant both aircraft would be better. The airlines and their customers benefited as a result.

By the end of the first jet decade, United had 110 DC-8's in its fleet, and Douglas had built 421 DC-8 units. Yet by the end of the first jet decade, United had become Boeing's biggest customer, with 220 Boeing-built jet planes in its service.

The first Boeing jet United bought was the 720, a smaller but improved version of the 707 with a new type of wing. The largest number of jet types United was ultimately to buy from anyone was the Boeing 727, and this aircraft was to become Boeing's most widely used jet of all types.

With the DC-8 and 720 suited to its longer routes, United wanted a smaller jet for intermediate use—say, New York-Chicago. There was none available in the U.S., and the manufacturers didn't show much interest in developing one. "We must become an all-jet airline," Patterson decided after a look at the initial experience with the big jets, and he sent a team of engineers to Toulouse, France, to look at the smaller 64-passenger twin-jet Caravelle that Sud Aviation was building. In February, 1960, United ordered 20 of the French planes, and the following year put them into service, initially on the New York-Chicago route. The Caravelles were immensely popular with the traveling public, and United's move galvanized Boeing's engineers into action.

The famed 727 trijet was the result. United placed an order for 40 of the 727's at the close of 1960. By the end of the first Jet Age, the company had 150 of the 727 types in its fleet and Boeing had built a total of 700, with its production line continuing at full speed. The 727 was as popular and widely used as the DC-3 and the DC-6 in their piston heydays.

By 1963 the conversion of United's fleet to jets had extended to the cargo field, as the company began the replacement of its piston freighters with the DC-8 freighter, which entered scheduled service the following year. Another development was the 727 QC—Q for "quick" and C for "convertible." The QC was a passenger plane by day, then its pallet-mounted seats and buffets could be removed through its wide doorway, and it was ready for cargo duty by night. In April, 1965, when United announced the industry's largest jet contract, calling for $750 million worth of DC-8's and 727's—75 units with options for 44 more—there were some QC type 727's in the package. The QC's did some yeoman service in the shorter haul cargo markets for years; but as larger combination passenger-cargo planes moved into such markets, they took over that role much more efficiently.

To complete its fleet conversion, United still needed another type, for short-haul passenger markets. There were two models available—one the Douglas DC-9, the other the Boeing 737. The Boeing and Douglas roles in the first jet years, when Boeing had the narrower 707 in prototype and Douglas the wider DC-8 on paper, were now reversed. The DC-9 was flying and Douglas had production orders for it, but its cabin was not wide enough for six-abreast coach seating. The 737 was in design and wooden mock-up stage only, but its cabin was the same diameter as the 707 and 727, and thus could easily accommodate six-abreast coach configuration. United carefully weighed the pros and the cons, and finally Patterson reached his decision; he was consistent, going with the wider cabin and the six-abreast seating arrangement.

The company ordered 75 Boeing 737's to set the stage for the completion of its first Jet Age reequipment program. As the plane went into service on the higher density traffic segments, the extra coach seats began to pay off. But even before it went into service, it had opened a veritable Pandora's box, with a problem that would bother the company for a long time.

Like the DC-9 (and the smaller British BAC-111 twin-engine jet which two U.S. trunk carriers bought for short-haul services), the 737 was designed and built for a two-pilot cockpit. However, there developed a difference of opinion within United concerning the safety factor of the 737 crew complement. During contract negotiations prior to the 737 entering scheduled service, the company's pilots requested a three-man crew on the basis that three pairs of eyes would be safer than two. The company did not agree that safety was an issue since the aircraft already had been evaluated as safe with a two-man crew.

The negotiation was protracted; the price to United of the extra flight crew member was estimated to be $6 million annually, based on 1968 costs and dollars. The issue was resolved with a compromise: there would be a six-month trial period during which the 737 would be operated with three men in the cockpit, but on 50 percent of the flights the third man would perform no duties. Then at the end of that time, the pilots' union committee and the company would evaluate the results and decide whether there should be two or three pilots. If they could not agree, the issue would be settled by an arbitrator.

Predictably, the company and the pilots could not agree. A board of arbitration decided the test should be extended for the duration of the contract, and if the parties then could not agree, the issue should be submitted to new arbitrators. Agreement was not reached; the issue again was submitted to arbitration and the second board further extended the three-man crew.

The DC-8's and the other jets brought a dramatic increase in speed, virtually doubling the 300-mile-per-hour average of the piston planes they replaced. They also brought a dramatic gain in economy, a benefit that would ultimately backfire in an unforeseen way.

The DC-8 could carry twice as many passengers as the DC-7, and with twice the speed could fly twice as far in a given time period. With the new jet's purchase cost of $6 million (triple the factory price of a DC-7) combined with its greater direct operating expense, the DC-8 airplane-mile operating cost was well above that of the DC-7, but its seat-mile cost was appreciably lower. Thus the Jet Age was ushered in with the welcome prospect of improved profits for the airlines which had long been striving for the 10.25 percent rate of return cited by the CAB as fair and reasonable. It appeared that the magic of jet economics would result in a new stability for the air transport industry. But the Bureau of Economics of the CAB was watching the improving bottom-line figures too, and it saw them as a lever to bring about lower fares for the traveling public. Technically the CAB had the power to disapprove fares, but not to initiate them. Practically the CAB had the muscle to force fare reduction, and on occasion it didn't hesitate to use that muscle.

As a hedge against the heavy amortization expenses of the costly jets as well as their substantial one-time introductory operating costs, the airlines had filed, and the CAB had approved, jet surcharges; these were additions of from $1.00 to $10.00 to the going piston fares on the segments being flown with the jets. But as the CAB's Bureau of Economics saw jet profits building up, it influenced the Board to stop approving newly filed surcharges and to demand a rollback of existing approved surcharges. This action would have had the desired effect of lowering passenger fares, but it would have cost the industry hundreds of millions in revenues and cut back its profit margin to the proverbial razor's edge.

Under severe pressure, United's marketing people developed the "Discover America" tariff, a 25 percent lower time-limited tourist coach fare structure applicable to the long periods of lean traffic volumes but "blacked out" during the peak summer and holiday periods. This unique tariff would give the Board what it wanted in lower fares, yet it promised to generate new travel for the carriers without discounting traffic during high demand times. United's marketers predicted accurately that the tariff would generate 30-35 percent in new revenues, more than offsetting the 25 percent cut; the CAB

91

reacted favorably and endorsed the revolutionary new tariff, dropping its threat of tariff rollbacks.

United's marketers had made another prediction about the "Discover America" discount: it would run out of its generative period in two or three years, after which it would decay into simply a discounted fare developing no offsetting new business. This prediction proved to be correct, and three years after its institution, the promotional and economic value of the plan had faded away.

But the pressure to keep fares low—and to make them lower—was kept on the airlines by the CAB, even to the point of forcing the trunks to give local service carriers a disproportionately higher share of interline ticket revenues in lieu of a higher rate of government subsidy to the small airlines. In some instances the local service carriers received amounts greater than the applicable local fare, resulting in the trunk carriers helping to furnish subsidies.

So airline yields from passenger tickets kept eroding through the decade of the first Jet Age, even after unit costs turned sharply upward. There occurred a lag of several years before the CAB permitted airline fare increases to become effective. Some congressional pressure for lower fares further delayed relief, and this proved to be one of the key factors in the cataclysmic losses to be sustained by United and other carriers commencing in 1970. Thus, a positive benefit of the early Jet Age had turned slightly sour, and the improvement in operating economics ushered in by the first jets was to be eroded by dropping yields.

In December, 1969, the company retired the last of its turboprop Viscount airplanes, and in February, 1970, United grounded the last of its piston-powered airplanes, and became a full jet airline.

Ten years after the DC-8 opened California-New York service, United's first Jet Age was completed, an age of the company's greatest growth and greatest investment. A total of 270 jet airplanes had been acquired at a cost of

$1.3 billion. In 1959, the opening year of the Jet Age, United carried 7.5 million passengers. In 1969, it carried 30 million passengers.

By that time the first of the second-generation jets— the huge, wide-bodied jumbos—were heading onto the production line.

Chapter 11

The United management team

W ith the postwar planning behind him, and with the jet fleets entering service, Patterson turned his attention to the people in higher management. The years had been as swift as they had been dynamic; now he must select his successor.

That task troubled him greatly. He hated the prospect of stepping out. United had long been his consuming interest, and it had become part of his fiber and soul. He also hated the thought that most of his key associates would not qualify to succeed him. He had seen too many railroad and other managements weaken and become erratic when chief executives were succeeded by contemporaries with only a few years to serve. He was one of the first business leaders to specify a span of 10-15 years of prospective service as a requirement of succession, and he knew this would rule out his closest associates.

In the technical area there had been Jack Herlihy, M.I.T. graduate and navy flyer, then a line pilot with old TAT, a TWA predecessor. Herlihy had long been Patterson's right hand in the operational technical side of the business. Brilliant yet painstakingly thorough, Herlihy's worth to United had been inestimable until death ended his aviation career.

William Mentzer had been Herlihy's key aide through those years, and he succeeded to the post of chief technical officer of the company. Mentzer was also a M.I.T. graduate, active in United's engineering group since

95

1930. His outstanding career was brought to an untimely close when he died shortly before his scheduled retirement.

Financial affairs of United were managed by Curtis Barkes, one of the most senior of all United people who had entered the service of National Air Transport in 1925. Barkes was very astute in matters of finance and carried the brunt of the tremendous financing programs through to the end of United's first Jet Age.

Marketing was first directed by Harold Crary, a veteran of promotion and merchandising that led to his founding of the Air Transport Association in 1928. Boeing selected Crary to head its promotion the following year, and in 1931 he went with Patterson to the Chicago headquarters of the newly formed United Airlines. Crary steered United's sales growth until he retired in 1953.

His successor was Robert E. Johnson, whom Crary had hired in March, 1929 and who had served in sales, advertising, and public relations capacities (except for war service as a naval air combat intelligence officer) until Crary's retirement.

Dick Petty, a long-time airman in United, was, following duty as an air force general in the war, Pat's senior flight officer for most of the postwar period. He directed the far-flung flight operations of the company until his retirement. He was succeeded by Gus Sommermeyer, another veteran airman who had a brilliant United career interrupted only by navy flight duty.

Russel F. Ahrens was an example of Patterson's technique of moving managers from one field to another. Ahrens, a veteran of the Boeing pioneering group, had come up through the sales organization when Pat spotted qualities in him that suited the requirements for personnel administration. For years until his retirement, Ahrens served as the company's personnel officer, an area in which Patterson himself was deeply involved.

Another key member of United's top management team was Hal Nourse, who had made his airline debut with Varney, which operated the Pacific Northwest route acquired by United. Patterson felt Nourse had been miscast in a public relations job, and converted him into an economic analyst and planner, a new classification in air transport's pioneering days.

When Nourse retired, he was succeeded by Andy de Voursney, a veteran with many years of United experience commencing as a reservations agent and moving up through the finance group to the post of treasurer, then top officer for economic planning.

Don Magarrell was retained as a consultant in the field of food services and became United's principal customer service officer. He established an unprecedented chain of flight kitchens on United, which became the foundation for the company's superior service.

A key postwar addition to United's top management group was Charles F. McErlean, brought in to direct the company's law department. Before Patterson's retirement McErlean had risen to the post of executive vice-president and general manager responsible for all of the operating functions of the company.

In its early days no airline had a medical department, relying on outside doctors to perform the physical examinations of pilots. Then Pat saw the value of company-wide preventive medicine, and persuaded Col. Arnold D. Tuttle, at that time director of the army's School of Aviation Medicine, to join United with the responsibility of establishing a full-fledged medical department. Upon Tuttle's retirement, he was succeeded by his assistant, Dr. George Kidera, who continued the preeminence of the company in that field in a most able manner.

There were others in the management picture over the years. Patterson had a penchant for spotting high potential among younger officers and promoting them to more demanding positions, working directly with him. Often these moves didn't work out and people would say that Patterson had become disenchanted. More often, the potential executive failed to survive the demanding pressure of higher responsibility.

In his search for a successor, Pat was candid with his group of senior officers. In the book *Pat Patterson,* the author Frank J. Taylor wrote:

"The officers were invited by Patterson to a dinner at Chicago's University Club. Everyone present sensed that something important was in the wind. It was. After a lively dinner, the genial host made a short talk which ended with the announcement that the next president of United Airlines would have to be at least 15 years younger than Patterson. There was silence as everyone looked around the table to mentally check the ages of those present, followed by a spontaneous laugh. At one swoop Patterson had eliminated everybody in United's top bracket of executives as presidential timber."

He gave no thought to looking beyond the company; he had brought managers from the outside into high-level posts and the majority of such cases ended in failure.

By 1962 Patterson had ended his search for his successor. He had settled upon George E. Keck, graduate of the University of Illinois, an army officer in World War II, and an industrial engineer for United. Keck had headed a project conducted by United with an outside firm to review some questions concerning the company's sprawling maintenance and engineering base at the San Francisco Airport. Should it continue to expand as a single huge plant, or should it be divided among two or more locations? How better could its organization be structured to carry out its steadily growing mission? When the survey was completed—and it recommended continuing the central concept but with a streamlined organization—Keck was named by Jack Herlihy to manage the complex base. He did that job well, so well, in fact, that his administrative abilities were evident not only to Herlihy, but to Patterson as well. And when it became apparent that the three basic operating groups— flight, customer services (transportation services was then the designation for ground and in-flight servicing activities), and maintenance and engineering—should be coordinated by a single executive, Keck was appointed. This would test his capacity; this would tell Patterson if the management consultants were right in saying Keck was far and away the best man to succeed him.

Keck was able, smart, ambitious, and tough. He had demonstrated his administrative abilities at the base, and he did so again in running the three operating divisions— so Patterson named him executive vice-president and general manager in 1962. A year later Pat was satisfied, and he recommended that the board of directors elect himself to a new post of chairman and chief executive officer and Keck to the presidency with the operating responsibility for the airline.

The move was made in the fall of 1963. Patterson occupied an executive suite office decorated in blue, his favorite color; Keck had a twin office in red. There was a connecting door between the offices, which was to be a symbol of the close relationship between the two.

For the next two years United experienced its greatest growth and earnings were good. The Jet Age planning was proving successful. Pat had passed the official company retirement age of 65 for officers and inside directors, and now he faced the hardest question of his career: with his successor functioning in his new role, why continue any longer as chief executive? After all, the directors had initiated an arrangement whereby he would serve as consultant for a period of ten years after he retired. He had a winter home in the southern California desert at Borrego Springs, and he was spending more and more time there during the severe Chicago winters. Why not turn over the full responsibility of his office to Keck? He spent several weeks at Borrego Springs wrestling with the problem. In essence, United Airlines was his life, and he knew what a loss to him it would be to put that life behind him. Yet he also knew there could be no halfway point for him. His presence in any capacity, even that of director, he decided, would inhibit his successor and would prevent him and his associates from freedom in directing the future United.

On the eve of a directors' meeting he discussed the wrenching decision with his wife—and Vera agreed he should cut the cord, cleanly and completely. Early the next morning he disclosed his decision to Curtis Barkes and Bob Johnson, and then walked into the board room and made his announcement, calmly and firmly. Despite the directors' urging, he did not budge from that decision. He would retire as chairman and director at the annual meeting of stockholders in 1966, and he did.

As the years went by, some would wonder if Pat had experienced second thoughts; if perhaps he might have regretted relinquishing his seat on the board which everyone wanted him to keep. No one but Pat would know that answer, but one can guess what a traumatic period of withdrawal he sustained. But he was right—there was no halfway point. Had he remained as chairman or even as a director, he would have continued to be "Mr. United" to many outside the company, and he surely would have continued to be Number One in the eyes of most employees.

On April 28, 1966, his last day as chief executive, Patterson was presiding over the shareholders' meeting when Director Gardner Cowles offered this resolution, which was accepted with a standing ovation:

"Few persons are granted the opportunity to participate in the shaping of an industry which is to affect profoundly the way of life of millions of people. Even fewer seize the opportunity when presented.

"It was a wise and providential fate which 40 years ago directed the steps of Vern C. Gorst, a pioneer commercial airline operator, to the desk of William A. 'Pat' Patterson in the Wells Fargo Bank of San Francisco. The vision and courage which in the ensuing years have marked Pat's every action were perhaps never more in demand when he approved a $5,000 loan to a United predecessor 40 years ago, a far more venturesome undertaking than his many multi-million-dollar decisions in recent years.

"Since that time, the eyes of Pat Patterson have been upon the stars, while his feet remained firmly on the ground. Always alert to the interests of his shareholders, he early recognized those interests could not be disassociated from the interests of the public which United served or of the employees who were its blood and bone. First and foremost in his thinking has been the safety of the passengers, regardless of cost or the effect on airline earnings. Second has been the welfare of United's employees from whom no complaint has ever been too trivial to merit his attention.

"Nothing the shareholders of United can do or say will add to the stature of the man who now steps down as chief executive of the world's greatest airline, but they cannot let this occasion pass without some expression of great affection and esteem for him.

"Now, therefore, be it resolved that the shareholders of United Airlines voice their pride in the company which Pat Patterson has created, their appreciation of the leadership which he has provided for a period of more than 30 years, and their hope that, relieved of the burden of executive responsibility, he may find that, for him, the best is yet to come."

After Pat left, George Keck had this to say:

"What makes this transition easy is that I am in perfect accord with the Patterson philosophy. His personal philosophy pervades this whole organization. It stands out among management and the people on the line. Pat has had a true and sincere belief that he had an obligation to people, whether customers or employees or stockholders. There is a universal respect for United Airlines on a worldwide basis. This is a great heritage to have. It stems from Pat; he created it. I'm going to carry on his philosophy and principles. I don't know any other."

Less than five years later, an embittered George Keck was gone from United.

The
Keck
years

1966–1970

George Keck *met the qualifications for the presidency which Patterson had laid out, including that of age — 50 years upon his election as president in 1963. Here were some of his attributes, which helped to cause a management consultant to identify Keck as "one of a half-dozen men throughout the country well qualified for any chief executive post."*

Analytical talent: Keck came to United in 1946 as an industrial engineer, a function he performed ably, in no small part because of his analytical talent. He was able to master the elements of a problem and to map the options for its resolution.

Deliberateness: He possessed a cool and objective temperament which enabled him to operate effectively in pressure situations. Whatever his inner emotions may have been, he was outwardly calm, and his decisions were reached deliberately. His German descent had bred thoroughness into his very fibers.

Caution: He was innately cautious, always making sure he had all the facts on both sides of a question before making a move. He would sacrifice time in favor of being completely sure of himself in most situations.

Toughness: Keck had the necessary degree of strength to be "hard-nosed" in his management technique. While some misinterpreted this trait to be callousness, it was simply the ability to be strongly firm when necessary.

Experience: Highly intelligent, Keck possessed com-

petence demonstrated through a series of demanding responsibilities as he moved up through the higher levels of airline management. He was well fortified by practical experience.

Ambition: He was motivated by an unusually strong drive to succeed. Ambition was one of his most impelling qualities.

Keck was not by nature a good communicator. He was reticent and lacked warmth of personality. He under- stood the importance of communication, and still con- siders that he communicated well, but there was a curtain of reserve between Keck and others that deterred free communication, and was to become a fatal flaw.

In appraising Keck's tenure in the United presidency, there is a factor which is intangible yet persuasive. Among the "Big Four" U.S. airlines, plus Pan American, no second-generation chief executive officer developed within his company has succeeded in the presidency of that company.

Just as United's evolution from a $3 million business to a billion-dollar corporation was guided by a great generalist and entrepreneur, so too were some of the bigger trunks: American by C. R. Smith, Eastern by Eddie Rickenbacker, Pan American by Juan Trippe. Differing in personality, these men nonetheless came from the same mold—they were bold, strong-minded, courageous, decisive leaders.

These were the first-generation managers who re- sponded to the challenge of building a whole new industry out of thin air, against the greatest of odds and the highest of risks. They were pure and unalloyed entre- preneurs. They were generalists. They surrounded them- selves with able associates—flying men, engineers, sales- men, accountants, and the rest; but when the chips came down, Patterson and the other leaders assessed their options and then made their decisions.

Whatever the reason—specialization, limited exposure to fundamental changes in top management techniques

106

throughout all businesses, the inhibiting shadow of the dominant predecessor who had gone but was not forgotten, or other possible reasons—these second-generation airline officials of the Big Four, plus Pan Am, did not last, and Keck was to be no exception.

The second jet age

From **1966** through 1969, the Keck regime achieved outstanding growth and good profits. The 1966 revenue total of $926 million was increased to $1.5 billion in 1969, and in the four-year period the aggregate net profit was over $200 million.

Keck and his management team not only saw to it that the day-to-day operations were conducted efficiently and profitably, but were responsible for the planning and decisions taken to the board of directors.

In the equipment field, these were years of paramount importance. The Boeing 747 and the Douglas DC-10 ushered in United's second Jet Age—the wide-bodied Jumbo Jet Age. This started off in a very promising way, but began to sputter before half a decade had passed by. Some people had seen danger in the 747 timing, but even with hindsight the peril probably could not have been avoided. The problem was simply that the 747 came too soon for its size, but two factors were to make it an inevitable buy for the airlines.

The problem started in 1964, when the air force put out specifications and sought bids for a huge cargo transport it designated as the C-5. There was strenuous competition among several aircraft manufacturers for what appeared then to be a contract plum of major dimensions. Lockheed won the competition and began to build what was by that time known as the C-5A.

Boeing had invested man-years and millions of dollars

in its C-5 design. When the award went to its competitor, Boeing recalled its earlier success in converting an air force tanker into the highly successful 707. So why not convert the freighter into a passenger plane? This is an extreme simplification of the premature birth of the 747, but in any event a subsonic jumbo jetliner with an advertised capacity of up to 490 passengers was formally offered for sale to the airlines.

The first of the factors that would make the 747 a reality was that Pan American, running true to its form of ordering just about any newly designed airliner, promptly bought 25, with options for another 10. The way was paved for the traditional domino effect as other carriers poised to follow Pan Am's suit.

The second factor was the availability of financing. The carriers were showing profits, the market was growing at an annual rate of 10 to 15 percent, new route franchises were being handed out, and the 747 with its abundance of seats was reflecting a big improvement in seat-mile operating costs. Consequently the airlines were able to sell equity in substantial amounts which in turn created the base for borrowing from banks and insurance companies.

Also on the equipment horizon was the SST—the British-French Concorde and the Boeing Supersonic 2727. The Anglo-French consortium was taking options at $100,000 a crack, and assigning delivery positions on a first-come basis. In the U.S. curiously, the FAA decided to quarterback option and delivery positions for the Boeing SST on the assumption that the government would bankroll the major developmental cost, but it ruled the prospective airline purchasers should put in some seed money at the rate of $1 million per unit ordered.

Keck and his equipment planning team took a cautious position in assessing the second Jet Age requirements. It was evident that the capacity of the 747 would be too big going into service—three times the number of seats of the jet it would replace. Never had a newly ordered transport plane been more than twice as large as the next previous airliner, and even so, there was usually an introductory period when the carrier "grew" its traffic into the new larger units. Of course, if it would be possible to replace the schedules of two DC-8's, say, with one 747, then the jump in size wouldn't be too difficult to manage. In any case, the question was really academic, for Pan Am's 747 order was followed by American and TWA. So with the dominoes falling, United felt impelled to order 25 units of the 747 type, later to be scaled down to 18, and with deliveries subsequently stretched out. When Pan Am, and then American and TWA, started service with their 747's, customers flocked to the initial schedules in great numbers, and the airplanes were plagued with start-up "bugs" in great numbers. United was hurt by the diversion of traffic from its narrow-bodied fleet until it got its 747's into service, but it benefited from the "de-bugging" of the 747 so that its initial operations were more reliable. The capacity impact began to be felt as more and more 747's were delivered and went into service. While the publicized 490-passenger capacity was never remotely attained, even the 360-seat configurations of the initial service planes soon proved much too large, and chunks of empty seats were replaced with spacious lounges for both coach and first-class passengers. The seat-mile cost of the 747 went up accordingly.

While competitors were signing up for SST options, United watched from the side, deliberating cautiously as it did with the 747. The only feasible use of the SST was long-range, and unless the sonic boom problem was solved to permit transcontinental operation, United's only possible market for supersonic operation was California-Hawaii. Eventually the company did take options for six Concordes with deliveries to begin several years after the first production aircraft, and it reserved positions for six U.S. SST's in similar down-line delivery spots.

The U.S. SST was doomed when the Senate refused to

underwrite the cost of the Boeing entry, and United and the other carriers ultimately got their deposits back. As the Concorde's economics and technical characteristics worsened, United cancelled its options and retrieved its deposits. Aside from the poor operating economics and the FAA's stated policy that no SST would be allowed to fly across the United States, another decisive stumbling block was the fact that no U.S. airline could borrow enough money to buy an SST even if it wanted to.

Meanwhile, Douglas and Lockheed looked at their futures and found their airline equipment orders threatened with extinction by the Boeing 747. Confronted with this unthinkable prospect, they found Boeing's vulnerability in the too-big size of its Jumbo, and both pressed tri-jet wide-bodied designs—the Douglas DC-10 and the Lockheed 1011. They were strikingly similar in appearance, and each would carry 250 passengers. The only real difference was in the power plant—the DC-10 using a G.E. engine and the 1011 using a Rolls Royce—and this would eventually turn out to be quite a difference.

United and American opted for the Douglas while Eastern and TWA went for the Lockheed, to be plagued with Rolls Royce's subsequent problems. Keck, like other airline executives, rued the unfortunate juxtaposition of the 747 and later, better-sized DC-10 and 1011.

The 747 was to become a popular airplane with air travelers, and it proved to be outstanding in operating efficiency and safety; but even five years after its debut, the 747's size still haunted some airlines, which mothballed some or all of their 747's when the 1974 fuel crisis forced reduction of schedule capacity. United did not have to ground 747's. It had the right number for its long-range markets, particularly California-Hawaii where the 747 proved to be most successful.

By the close of 1969, United was well into its Second Jet Age, and two significant facts were becoming clear: first, the sharp improvement in operating economies which characterized the First Jet Age were conspicuously absent; and second and more important, both the first and the second generation jets would have a longer useful life than originally anticipated. When the DC-8's and 707's entered service, their great increases in speed and size had combined to cause a significant gain in productivity, but this was not the case with the jumbo jets. There was no gain in the subsonic speed, so this element of the equation was missing; furthermore, first generation jet operating costs had long since overtaken initial economies. The seat-mile costs of the 747 were appreciably lower then the narrow-bodied aircraft, but load factors dropped so this potential economy was academic. The smaller sized DC-10's and 1011's were an improvement over the 747 in airplane mile costs, but their potential economy of performance was also diluted because of lower loads.

The really optimistic aspect of the Second Jet Age was the stability United could foresee in a new freedom from technical obsolescence of aircraft which had been such a financially disruptive factor over the years. With the SST out of the picture, and with no bigger and better subsonic jets in prospect, United and the other trunk carriers could envision at least 10 or 15 years with the jumbos and the 727-class smaller jets fulfilling their principal aircraft requirements. Now they would have the opportunity seldom present in the past to work their fleets with improving profitability as they amortized their large investments.

The manufacturers recognized the new situation when, after a halfhearted and abortive verbal pass or two at future 1,000-passenger jets, they adapted themselves to stretching out the production lines of existing jets and converting narrow-bodied aircraft to the "advance wide-bodied look."

The farther into the future the Second Jet Age could be extended, the better for the U.S. carriers.

Chapter 13

Crisis and the CAB

The air transport industry has always been under some form of government regulation, but never did this have such an effect upon United as during Keck's presidency.

When the government established the airmail routes in the twenties and then turned them over to private companies through competitive bidding, it recognized that the development and maintenance of commercial air transportation was the province of the private enterprise system. But it also knew that government regulation of routes and prices would be a continuing necessity for the protection of the public as well as for the good of the industry itself to avoid self-destruction. So there has been a partnership between the federal government and the airline industry down through the years.

In the case of United Airlines—and indeed other carriers as well—this partnership has not always been happy and amicable. From time to time the CAB has seemed to step out of its regulatory role into some airline management area considered to be a carrier prerogative. On such occasions when United would be affected, the company would speak out quite forcefully, first through Pat Patterson whose effectively sharp ripostes would sometimes take the form of paid advertisements (as for example, when the Board laid down specifications for aircraft coach seating configurations), and later through George Keck who was following his predeces-

115

sor's example of criticizing CAB actions that appeared damaging.

As recently as early 1974, *Fortune* magazine pointed an accusing finger at both the CAB and the carriers on their joint record of poor performance:

"The 180 million passengers who traveled last year on 50,000 city-to-city routes throughout the U.S. paid about 6 cents per mile—a price that is only about 12 percent higher in current dollars than in 1958 when the first commercial jet aircraft were introduced.

"In achieving that performance, the airlines and the Civil Aeronautics Board have lived up admirably to only half of the aims of the 1938 Civic Aeronautics Act, which created the government framework for our air transport system. Such a system, said the law, should further the public 'right' to travel by air 'through adequate, economical, and efficient service . . . at reasonable charges.' But the congressional mandate also called on the system to foster 'sound economic conditions' and to operate without 'undue preferences,' 'advantages,' or 'unfair or destructive practices.' In carrying out this half of Congress' intent, the airlines and their regulators have failed miserably."[1]

Two CAB actions were taken during Keck's regime which would have a profound effect upon United—the final decision in the transpacific route case in 1969, and the institution of a general passenger fare investigation in 1970. The first was to help plunge United deeply into the red within a year because of the disastrous diversion of revenues to the new competitors which flooded the Hawaiian market. The second threatened to slow the remedial rate increases the airline industry required to narrow the widening gap between costs and prices.

Recognizing the perilous lag in the cost-price ratio, Keck's management acted to obtain passenger fare increases, but it was not until early 1969 that the CAB gave

1. Michael B. Rothfeld, "New Downdrafts for the Airlines." *Fortune* (January, 1974).

permission, then only for a 3.8 percent increase, the first since 1962 during which period the cost index had increased by 9.6 percent. Some of the CAB's reluctance reflected congressional pressures to hold down the fare levels. Toward the end of the year the CAB did respond to the carriers' need for fare relief by granting a 5.6 percent increase. But this was conditioned on a demand that the trunk carriers accept a joint-fare formula which would materially reduce their share of local service joint revenues in favor of the smaller lines. The trunks opposed this pressure tactic, but the CAB was adamant and obtained grudging agreements from the trunks, one by one. Keck held out until the eleventh hour, and United was the last trunk carrier to give in. Ironically, litigation initiated by a congressman succeeded in blocking this increase, and distracted the CAB from prompt action to help the airlines.

To deal with the fare problems, the CAB initiated a general investigation of domestic passenger fares and related matters. In 1960 the CAB had conducted a similar investigation, and concluded that as a matter of policy, a trunk airline was entitled to a 10.25 percent rate of return on investment. The 1970 investigation would ultimately find that a trunk airline would be entitled to a 12 percent rate of return, although the Big Three transcontinental airlines had seldom achieved the 10.25 percent rate fixed 10 years earlier.

The transpacific route case is an extreme example of the damage which the CAB can inflict upon the industry in the long and painful absence of a basic national air transportation plan (which United has been advocating since 1940). *Fortune* said in its January, 1974 issue:

"The Civil Aeronautics Board, has failed to follow any thoughtful, logical, or consistent policy in awarding routes. The carriers have generally applied for as many routes as they figured they could get, and the CAB has usually obliged them without much consideration of the long range economic considerations. We've gone through feasts of route awards, admits one high CAB official. Now we have to deal with the indigestion.

"The most notorious case involves the Mainland-Hawaii run, once served only by United, Pan American, and Northwest. In 1969, the Board let five more carriers compete for Hawaii traffic. At least five of the eight lines serving the Islands complain that they generally lose money on Hawaii flights."[2]

The transpacific case caused a disastrous swing in United's net profit on its Hawaiian operation alone from a plus $19 million in 1969 to a minus $17 million in 1970 and was a major factor in the company's total 1970 plunge into the red. In addition to ignoring economic consequences as charged by *Fortune,* the Board passed over the fact that United is the nation's largest "local service airline" operating to many small points without the subsidy granted the local service carriers, and is dependent upon profits from such long-haul routes as Hawaii to offset small city losses.

The CAB has emphasized that no route award was ever made without some carrier asking for it, which was certainly so in the Transpacific Case. Every U.S. trunk airline applied for a Hawaiian franchise, one subsequently withdrew, and the Board granted about half the applications.

The "Transpac" route case commenced back in 1959, and in 1960 the CAB found that one additional carrier—Western Airlines—should be granted the route, all other applicants being denied. But rather than settled, the case was just beginning. At the request of President Eisenhower, the award was withheld, and the case remanded to the CAB for review in 1961. In 1963 the Board terminated the case and all applications were denied.

While Hawaiian traffic continued to burgeon, United, Pan Am, and Northwest more than kept pace with the market growth, and maintained sufficient service that on

2. *Ibid.*

an annual average, nearly twice as many seats were provided as passengers carried. Nevertheless, the hue and cry from other carriers intensified; and in 1965 the Board opened a new Transpacific Case, again looking at Hawaii as well as points west: Tokyo, Hong Kong, Manila, Sydney, and Auckland, among many. United prepared to defend its Mainland-Hawaii position and also applied for routes west of Honolulu to Australia and New Zealand (later withdrawn because of its doubtful economics) and to Japan.

In December, 1968, President Johnson approved the numerous awards in the case. Three days after his inauguration in January, 1969, President Nixon rescinded the route awards and sent them back to the Board for further consideration. Six months later, Nixon approved the CAB's revised awards, and except for some futile court action, the case was finally settled. A wave of new airlines threatened to engulf Hawaii, and barrels of red ink began to be rolled out.

In no route proceeding in its history did United work so hard to present its case—and to no avail. Small armies of airline witnesses paraded rosy forecasts before the CAB examiner, and the Board itself was caught up in the euphoria of repeated 15 percent annual industry traffic growth records. Because of its size, the CAB found United (by far the biggest in the Hawaii market) could afford to have its Mainland-Hawaii traffic decimated by the influx of new competition. And also because of its size, United should not be considered for a new route to the Far Pacific, because such an award would only make United that much bigger.

The Transpacific Case also illustrates the action and reaction of this phase of the regulatory process as it affects total airline capacity—and overcapacity.

In its long-range equipment planning, United, like Pan American and Northwest, was mindful of its obligation to provide demonstrably adequate service to the Islands, as well as to continue the development of a profitable market. The CAB was watchful of carrier performance in all markets and quick to point out pressure situations when load factors might climb above the area of 65 percent. Thus as early as 1965 United ordered a number of the high-capacity, long-range DC-8-61's for Hawaii operation, and in 1966 ordered 747's, earmarking 10 for the Hawaiian market.

Within a year of the transpacific route awards, the company placed the first of its 747's in service to the Islands. Immediately upon receiving their Hawaiian routes, some of the newcomers had rushed to buy 747's or other aircraft for that run with the inevitable consequence of overcapacity. (Within four years one newly certified carrier to Hawaii had mothballed its 747 fleet when the energy crisis put a premium on frequency and a penalty on overcapacity.) In almost every competitive route case of any size, the existing operators have provided future expansion of capacity for serving the market and its growth, and the newcomers have bought new life to serve the same markets; hence, because of the long lead time in equipment planning and deliveries, route awards often lead directly to potential overcapacity, and the harassed carriers create another problem for themselves.

There are those who feel the Transpacific Case was the CAB's "last hurrah." After the Hawaiian roof fell in upon carriers and the CAB alike, further route awards were frozen. The situation was described in the memorable words of the then Board Chairman Secor Browne: "Ain't nobody going to get nothing!" It is quite probable that this painful lesson will be long remembered by the carriers and the Board alike; yet some observers recall the smaller scale route spree of 1955 when Chairman Ross Rizley and his fellow Board members distributed so many new routes that there followed a period of indigestion quite similar to that cited by the "high CAB official" quoted in the January, 1974 issue of *Fortune* magazine.

One premise does seem valid: in the perennial carrier-

CAB route equation, it should be the CAB's responsibility to administer with discretion because of its responsibility for economic stability in the industry. Every airline has a department with one or more people paid to figure out what its next route application should be, and every "have-not" airline is dedicated to the proposition that its one sure avenue to a "have" status is through route expansion. The notion of self-restraint in route aspirations among airlines is heartily applauded by each carrier, just as long, of course, as that self-restraint doesn't apply to itself.

Irrespective of logical and philosophical arguments, the Transpacific Case was perpetrated, and Keck and his associates were justifiably outraged at the results which were to prove so costly to the company. Keck has always felt that the CAB should bear the major responsibility for "the deteriorization of the industry's health" in general and United's financial ills in particular. While he readily conceded some of the problems "were in part due to management errors of decision and faulty judgment," he is convinced the "CAB ignored its basic charge to foster a sound, healthy industry." In Keck's opinion, the company suffered along with the industry because "the Board's position on rates and tariffs was dilatory, unwise, and hostile to the carriers." He resented the "CAB pressure to reduce fares when the industry had a prime opportunity through jet efficiency to attain a strong financial position" and to approach the 10.25 percent rate of return on investment conceded to be reasonable by the CAB. He felt the threat to roll back jet surcharges, which would have cost the industry an estimated $200 million and more annually and which was averted only by United's "Discover America" tariff, was "an act of unlawful coercion."

This is why Keck, in the Patterson manner, spoke out against the CAB, strongly and openly, for United indeed had been badly wounded by the Transpacific Case and by tardy fare relief.

Chapter 14

The birth of UAL, Inc.

U nited Airlines was sired by a holding company in 1931, five years after its predecessor airlines had started flying their routes. United found itself the junior member of an aviation family that included four airplane manufacturers, an aircraft engine plant, a builder of helicopters, a maker of propellers, and two airports. United Aircraft and Transport Corporation was the largest and most diversified of the several aviation conglomerates, and it became a target of the federal government during the aftermath of the airmail cancellations of 1934, when the Roosevelt Administration decided to split up the holding companies and decreed that in the future airlines would be just airlines.

So United Airlines became independent as strictly an air carrier (along with the ownership of Union Air Terminal at Burbank which was later sold to Lockheed Aircraft for its World War II expansion).

That was one reason why the company confined itself solely to air transportation during the next three decades. Another was that its own surging growth through those years absorbed all of its financial resources and management talents. Its corporate philosophy was clear: stick to operating the airline for that's a full-time job and then some. Other airlines followed the same course.

But during these decades related businesses grew up around the airlines and the airports: rental cars, originated as a service unconnected with air travel but becoming successful because of it; airport motels, and subsequently airport hotels; restaurants at and around air terminals; food catering to serve airlines; even moving pictures and soft music. In years when carriers went into the red, frustrated airline managers wondered if they were becoming profitless transporters of customers who supported profitable satellite businesses, as they watched their low-priced economy seats fill up with travelers who would deplane at their destinations and check into high-priced hotel accommodations and seek out expensive restaurants.

It was the hotel business which first took the airlines beyond their basic role, when Pan American set up its Inter-Continental Hotel system around the world, followed by TWA's acquisition of the international wing of the Hilton chain. And it was the hotel business which attracted United's interest in broadening its scope of operations. Pan Am had gone into hotels mainly for the reason that many of its foreign destinations lacked adequate quality accommodations acceptable to American tourists. TWA acquired the Hilton International group as a competitive countermeasure which it correctly estimated would be profitable. United decided to get into the domestic hotel field to capitalize on a profit opportunity in a closely related business.

In 1967 the company made five-year projections which showed a continued annual growth rate between 10 and 15 percent. The company's marketing group felt it saw both an opportunity and a need to move into the hotel business. It commissioned Harris, Kerr, Forster—hotel management consultants—to study the relationship between air transport and hotel industries and what United should be doing about it. The HKF people did a comprehensive analysis focused on a half-dozen key United markets. In 1968 it recommended that United enter the hotel field for several reasons: a substantial percentage of hotel guests in cities such as Chicago, Los Angeles, New York, San Francisco, Honolulu and others traveled to and from those points on United's planes; demand for hotel rooms could exceed the supply of existing and projected hotel rooms in certain markets, and ownership of hotel properties could prove an important hedge against unavailability of hotel space; and there was a substantial profit opportunity. The consultants offered several avenues for United to consider, ranging from building new hotels, to buying existing properties, to acquiring a fullblown hotel chain with competent management expertise. In due course the board of directors approved the recommendations in principle.

At this point there arose the basic question of how a hotel venture might best be undertaken organizationally. Should it be a division of the airline itself, or should it be operated separately? Even more crucial was the question of whether United should go further into other fields of business and industry to increase the corporation's profitability and to help offset the cyclical fluctuations in its financial profile.

The answer was in favor of diversification beyond the hotel business. To keep such a program from getting mixed up with the basic job of running an airline, it appeared desirable to establish a holding company to be the corporate vehicle to accomplish that objective.

A series of legal steps was begun in December, 1968, and approved by the stockholders in April, 1969, which resulted in the incorporation of UAL, Inc. as a holding company with United Airlines as a wholly-owned subsidiary. At the April, 1969, shareholders' meeting the philosophy underlying the move was set forth:

"The basic purpose of UAL, Inc., is the acquisition or formation of subsidiaries which will increase United's profitability. Generally speaking, new enterprises will be related to and will support our primary business of air transportation. The goal of UAL, Inc., will be to develop itself in endeavors which will stabilize the earnings of the overall enterprise. We propose to enter into businesses which are not affected by cyclical factors as our basic business, air transportation. Our goal is to develop or acquire businesses which will create better debt/equity relationship for the enterprise and stabilize earnings capability. Achievement of this goal will enable UAL, Inc., to raise funds in the marketplace on a more favorable basis than is available to the airline industry alone."

By August, 1969, the CAB had given the reorganization plan a green light on the basis it did not involve CAB jurisdiction, and the Internal Revenue Service had given its approval of the financial details of the plan which provided for an even exchange of United Airlines stock for an equal number of UAL, Inc. stock. The plan was implemented with United's outside directors forming the UAL, Inc. board (while remaining as directors of the operating subsidiary as well), with George Keck elected to be president of both UAL, Inc., and United Airlines, and Curtis Barkes vice-president. (In later years the following officers were added to UAL, Inc.'s management: Vice-presidents Irvin Williamson, Norbert Kraegel, Ralph Robertson, Irving Roth, and Secretary E. O. Fennell. Keck was to be replaced by Edward Carlson, and Barkes became chairman of UAL's finance and audit committees upon his retirement.)

Thus United Airlines had come full circle. It had started out life as a holding company subsidiary, and now three and one-half decades later, it was again a holding company subsidiary, but with one great big difference—it had become a billion-and-a-half-dollar business in the meantime, and it was the only subsidiary its holding company owned.

As the reorganization developed, the matter of entry into the hotel field could be pursued in earnest. The first moves were made on tiptoe: participation in the development and operation of the Stanford Court Hotel in San Francisco, and agreement with AMFAC for joint ownership and operation of the 500-room Waikiki Beachcomber in Honolulu. While these were good moves, it was obvious that it would take a long time to make a significant dent in the hotel business. So attention turned to the HKF recommendation to acquire a hotel chain.

There were—and are—a number of fine hotel systems in the United States. One appeared to be particularly well suited to team up as a partner in travel with United Airlines. Western International Hotels had management or ownership interest in 71 hotels in 14 countries, but 78 percent of its total rooms were in cities directly served by United Airlines. Furthermore, its philosophy and policies were compatible with those of United, there was a rapport between the top managements, and WIH was a profitable operation in itself. So UAL, Inc. went back to Seattle, United's one-time home, to pay court to Western Hotels. The result was to prove more far-reaching than anyone could have suspected.

The
Carlson
years

1971–

The Carlson era *officially commenced on December 21, 1970. It is said that Edward E. Carlson was brought in "to turn United around, to get it back into the black." That was only part of the reason. A turnaround was vitally important in the short term, but Carlson's prime mission was to change the company's basic direction, which was essential in the long term.*

When George Keck said in 1966 that he would "carry on Patterson's philosophy and principles, I don't know any other," he unknowingly put his finger on his future problem, for times were changing and ways of managing had to change with them.

That was why the UAL, Inc. board found it necessary to change top management in December, 1970. By that time the problems which confronted the company had been identified and solutions were being sought, perhaps too late, and too slowly. Nevertheless, the approaches had been undertaken: unilateral schedule reductions; the first attempt of United, American, and TWA to enter into mutual capacity reductions (which the CAB initially denied); payroll cuts; capital plans reduced or eliminated, and similar actions. Such approaches were intensified in 1971 and 1972 to bring United into the black.

But the root causes remained: the unwieldy, monolithic organization; the practice of management promotion by seniority, step by step; the ingrained ways of doing things as they had always been done — the continu-

ation of management as it had been, not necessarily adjusted to changes; the slowness to act and react; the failure to communicate. These were the elements of the problem which confronted Carlson.

Why Carlson? What attributes for leadership in a new direction did he have?

Carlson is like Patterson is some ways, different in others. He is small in stature, possesses the same trait of boldness as Patterson, and he too has innate caution which he uses to good advantage. Among others, he also holds several beliefs which combine to make him a most effective leader in the new mold of corporation executives:

Profit Consciousness: Eddie Carlson preaches the profit-center concept; he preaches it well because he is a profit center in himself. He understands that the foremost requisite of business success in the free enterprise system is to make a profit, and his first priority is black ink on "the bottom line, after taxes."

Dynamism: He is dynamic in the complete sense. He is a man of action, and action now. He is comfortable in a dynamic environment — the only fields he has been involved with are the businesses of hotels and air transportation, both with continual movement. He is a driver. He is compulsively so, and he drives himself much harder than he drives others.

Change: He believes what is poor should be good, what is good should be better, and what is better should be excellent. He believes what is good enough for today will not be so tomorrow. He believes in change — change to meet new conditions, change to foster new developments. He is impatient, and wants each minute and every movement to count.

Accountability: Carlson is a strong advocate of accountability, demanding that his managers be accountable for results. He delegates, but he also audits performance closely.

Generalism: He believes that a top-flight manager can

132

manage anything within a business framework. He believes a specialist may end up with blinders, unperceptive to other vital elements of the whole; at the same time he knows that good specialists are essential to an organization. He looks at younger managers as possible future executives, and when they respond by demonstrating their potential, he wants to see them moved across the spectrum of management.

Communication: *Carlson is a confirmed communicator. He places great reliance upon the committee system of management as an effective approach to decision making, but more important, as a sure-fire system of communications.*

People Orientation: *Just as Carlson is profit conscious, he is people perceptive. He was successful in the hotel field because he was highly sensitive to the human equation, and he is successful in air transportation for the same reason, for both are people businesses in the most intense way.*

Carlson has other qualities: he is ambitious, determined, hard-nosed, sometimes oblique and yet often bluntly direct, loyal to those who are loyal to him, quickwitted, at times surprisingly compromising. But the attributes listed above—along with a proven track record of success in modern management—are why the UAL board selected him to lead United. They are the factors which enabled him to accomplish such far-reaching changes in the first three Carlson years with United. They are what make Eddie run.

The story of Western Hotels

U nited Airlines traces its corporate antecedents
back to 1925, to the four pioneer airlines which
were combined to form United in 1931. The
names of the predecessor companies have long since
disappeared, but their routes still form the backbone of
United's present system.

Western International Hotels traces its corporate antecedents back to 1910, even back to 1893. Of the first 26
hotels in its chain—or "family" as Western prefers it—
only one remains, an appendix of the Washington Plaza
in Seattle.

Since its incorporation Western has owned, operated,
managed, or represented a total of 78 hotels in the U.S.
and Canada. Of these, 57 are no longer members of the
group. As of this writing, the Western flag flies over 55
hotels in diverse parts of the world: the U.S. and Canada, of course, and Mexico, Central America, the Far
East, Australia, South Africa, and Europe. Eight are
under construction and many more are on the drawing
boards.

Western Hotels became an incorporated organization
in August, 1930, just one year prior to United Airlines'
formation. Like United, Western was an amalgamation
of companies owned and operated by several different
groups. They were Severt W. Thurston and Harold
Maltby, hotel operators in Seattle; Frank A. Dupar, a
contractor who built hotels in Washington; and Adolph

and Peter Schmidt, who had gone into the hotel business in Olympia and Seattle when prohibition temporarily stymied their Olympia brewery operations.

It all started way back in October, 1893, when a saw-mill operator named Maltby from Lynden, Washington, bought the 101-room National Hotel in Seattle, and his son, Harold Maltby, assisted in operating the hotel until 1910. In that year an acrobat named Severt W. Thurston decided to give up his precarious stage career and got a job as a bellboy in that same National Hotel. Maltby and Thurston became close friends and decided to go into the hotel business on their own, forming the Maltby-Thurston Corporation in 1910. They converted an old building to a hotel, and were off and running, taking over old hotels, refurbishing them, and operating them profitably. As they prospered, they acquired the large but old Lincoln Hotel in Seattle; and in renovating it, added a brand new feature for that time—a telephone in every room. Maltby and Thurston had borrowed $160,000 to complete the remodeling, and their investment looked good for a few days—until the hotel was destroyed by fire in which several guests lost their lives and all lost their personal belongings. The next morning Severt Thurston went to his bank and said: "I don't want you to be concerned about our note—we will pay it off as soon as we can." Even though they were not legally liable, Thurston and Maltby compensated their guests for their losses. Thus, although the fire was a short-term setback, the reputation of Thurston and Maltby for complete integrity was firmly established and that integrity was to become a cornerstone of Western Hotels' corporate philosophy.

By the summer of 1930, the Thurston-Maltby team had expanded by adding a few more hotels, and Thurston went to Yakima, Washington, to see about a proposed new hotel. There he encountered Frank A. Dupar, who was on the same mission. Dupar had started out in the plumbing business and then, as a contractor, had built and was operating hotels in Seattle and in eastern Washington. The two discussed the hotel business which, in that first depression year, was having its problems. Out of the conversation came the notion of joining forces, and in addition, linking up with the Schmidts and their hotels. The idea was that benefits might come from stabilizing rates, standardizing accounting procedures, pooling purchases, and sharing reservations systems. There was strong interest among the three parties, but no agreement could be reached as to the values of each other's hotels. So the outcome was the formation of Western Hotels as a management company, owning no stock in the hotel properties, but coordinating policies and performing management services at appropriate fees for the 18 original hotels, all in the state of Washington.

On August 28, 1930, Western Hotels was incorporated as a management company with Thurston as president, Maltby as vice-president, Dupar as secretary, and Adolph and Peter Schmidt among its directors, and with its headquarters in Seattle. (Just eleven months later, United Airlines was incorporated also as a management company, with its headquarters being moved from Seattle to Chicago.)

Western was actually a federation of independently owned hotels and for a while it continued to operate as such, with the corporation itself having little or no equity in the hotel properties it managed. Yet from the beginning there was a high degree of policy direction and control of service standards, always a great asset.

During the next decade Western added 10 more hotels, and significantly four were outside the State of Washington: the Georgia in Vancouver, B.C.; the Multnomah in Portland, Oregon; the Boise in Idaho; and a key acquisition, the Sir Francis Drake in San Francisco. The deal for the latter hotel was negotiated, but not consummated, on December 5, 1941; then came Pearl Harbor and the great uncertainties which were immediately created. What should Western do about the Drake? Thurston had the answer: "Let's go through with the deal anyway. If we go down, we'll all go down together; if we rise, we'll rise together!'' This was a landmark deal for Western, and it moved into the hotel big league.

Even greater an asset for Western than its policies and service standards has been its people, commencing with Thurston and Dupar. Severt Thurston guided Western Hotels from its inception in 1930 for three decades, and he was in great part responsible for its initial growth. His attributes were many: complete integrity, dedication, coolness and wisdom, a strong profit orientation, a keen judgment of people, and an abiding conviction that hard work is an essential ingredient of success. He was serious-minded, and while he had a dry sense of humor, he was not particularly imaginative. His associates like to tell such anecdotes as the one about Mrs. Thurston, who, seeing her husband appear in a familiar blue suit, suggested it might be time for him to buy some new clothes, only to have him reply, ''What's the matter? This *is* a new suit; I just bought it a few days ago.'' This story suggests why for years Western Hotels were invariably refurbished in the same conservative color schemes. There's also the story about Thurston being invited to attend an office Christmas party, and when he arrived with the crowded affair in full swing, grasped the arm of an associate and asked in alarm: ''Surely we don't have all these people on our payroll, do we?'' A few left Western's employment shortly thereafter.

Thurston knew how to pick management people. From its first staff of officers 45 years ago, Western's top and middle managers have been developed from within the organization. Eddie Carlson is obviously the number one example, but there have been many others:

Lynn Himmelman, the son of Troy Himmelman who was a Western Hotel pioneer and long-time officer-director, started at the bottom rung, climbed to the executive vice-presidency by 1960, and succeeded Carlson as chief executive officer at the end of 1970 when Carlson moved out to run United Airlines and UAL, Inc.

138

Gordon Bass began his Western career in the early thirties, reached an executive vice-presidency by 1965, became president in 1971 when Himmelman assumed the chairmanship, and moved up to become vice-chairman at the close of 1973.

Harry Mullikin entered Western's service in 1943 and got his big opportunity when Western joined with Alcoa to develop the Century Plaza in Los Angeles in 1963. Mullikin was appointed vice-president in charge of developing the Century Plaza, and he brought it on line in 1966. Mullikin became executive vice-president in 1971, and president in 1973.

There are other Western names great in hotel history: Dan London (synonymous with the St. Francis and San Francisco), Willard Abel, and many others.

But the leadership of Thurston during the formative years, and Carlson during the expansion years was the dominant force in Western's emergence as one of the principal hotel groups in the world.

Interestingly, Carlson's hotel career had the same beginning as Thurston's: both started as bellboys. While going to the University of Washington, Carlson worked part-time and during summer vacations as a page boy at Western's Benjamin Franklin Hotel, followed by experiences as elevator operator and bellhop. By 1932, he found himself unable to afford to continue his college courses, so he dropped out and decided to go into business for himself selling hat-blocking equipment. When that venture foundered, Carlson decided to go back to the hotel business, and he got a job as a room clerk in Western's Roosevelt Hotel. Within four years he had worked his way up to assistant manager, then was appointed manager of the President Hotel in Mt. Vernon, Washington. In 1937 he was offered the managership of Seattle's exclusive Rainier Club where he stayed until entering the U.S. Naval Reserve in 1941. During those four years at the club, he became well acquainted with many of Seattle's top business and civic leaders, associations which would prove most valuable to him in his postwar career. In fact, during that period, Carlson was offered a job by United Airlines as a salesman, an offer which was flattering but financially unattractive.

On his return from service in 1946, he had his choice of three jobs: assistant to President Thurston of Western Hotels at $6,000 a year; his old job at the Rainier Club at $12,000; a managerial post with the Olympic Hotel (at that time under different management) in Seattle at $18,000. Eddie Carlson unhesitatingly chose the job with Thurston. Within ten years he was executive vice-president and Western had acquired the Olympic. By 1960 Carlson was president and chief executive officer, with Thurston (then age 70) moving up to chairman. Five years later Thurston decided to retire and to sell out to Western his equities in various of the hotel properties.

Soon after the war, Eddie Carlson had put into practice a management technique he has used effectively since then—a closely knit management committee to coordinate planning and policy decisions. Lynn Himmelman and Gordon Bass became key members of Eddie's group, and the triumvirate operated closely for the next 30 years.

Expansion continued at a steady pace, with hotels both new and old, large and small, being added to the Western family. Some were tested for long-term profitability and found wanting, and these eventually were to be dropped; others were keystone properties and would remain under the Western flag. There were the Benson in Portland, the St. Francis, The Olympic, Vancouver's Bayshore Inn, the Continental Plaza, the Century Plaza, and the Washington Plaza.

Carlson not only became a prominent businessman, he played a major role as a civic leader. One of his many community activities was serving as chairman of the citizen's committee that planned and operated the highly successful Century 21 Exposition, the 1962 World's Fair which left the community a splendid complex of civic buildings. For this work, he was named Seattle's first citizen in 1966. And though he had to drop out of the University of Washington before he could complete the curriculum, the University named him alumnus *summa laude dignatus* in June, 1970.

Two fundamental changes in policy initiated by Carlson toward the end of the fifties had a great influence on Western's future: one strengthened the company's equity in the properties it partially owned or managed; the other expanded the geography of its operations, reflecting the shrinking of intercontinental distances brought about by the Jet Age.

The company turned from its philosophy of managing an affiliated string of hotel properties having a variety of ownership situations, to a consolidation of the direct and indirect ownerships into a single corporation, resulting in a stronger corporate and financial structure for the parent company. At the same time Western reaffirmed its long-range policy of developing new hotel facilities, preferably with strong partners.

Alert to the coming impact of jet air travel, Western lifted its geographic sights and commenced expansion into America's neighboring countries to the north and south. In Canada there came the Bayshore Inn in Vancouver, the Calgary Inn, the Bonaventure in Montreal, the Winnipeg Inn, the Edmonton Plaza, and soon to follow, a major hotel in Toronto.

In Mexico Carlson teamed up with investor/hotelier Jose Brockmann, and now Western operates 20 units in that country, plus some in Guatemala and the Camino Real in San Salvador.

In the Far East, Western has hotels in Japan, Hong Kong, Bangkok, and Singapore; and it is affiliated in Sydney, Australia, with the excellent Wentworth.

Europe has not offered many opportunities as yet for Western, but the company is in partnership with Scandinavian Airlines in operating the new Scandinavia in Copenhagen, and a hotel is under construction in Oslo, also

141

in cooperation with S.A.S. Far to the south, Western operates the new Carlton Hotel in Johannesburg.

But its main expansion program is within the United States, where Western is making a major addition to the Century Plaza as it has to the Continental Plaza and the St. Francis; and where it has recently spread its flag to Texas with the Houston Oaks, to Kansas City with the impressively new Crown Center, to Washington, D.C. with the Mayflower, Honolulu with acquisition of the Ilikai (in which it formerly had an equity), and with new hotels under construction in Detroit and Southfield, Michigan; Costa Mesa, California; and in Atlanta, Georgia. New York City has long been a bright glint in Western's eyes, and for one year it operated the famous Savoy Plaza, until it was displaced by an office building. Efforts to reenter New York via the World Trade Center and an older midtown hotel failed to materialize. But now Western has a dramatic future New York entry with the forthcoming John Portman-designed superhotel announced for opening in the late seventies. It is also involved with Portman in a new major hotel to be constructed in the next few years in downtown Los Angeles.

One measure of Western's successful expansion is the record of gross revenues, doubling from 1965's $45 million to 1970's $90 million, while net earnings rose in the same period from $750,000 to $3 million. Another measure is the fact that Western's standard of hospitable and personalized service has been instilled and maintained among the personnel in all the properties it operates. Western chose to identify this service quality as "The House of Friendship."

In its long-range planning, Western saw itself as a self-sufficient, corporately independent organization. The only change was in its corporate name, from "Western Hotels" to "Western International Hotels." In the company's 1969 annual report, Carlson had this to say about Western's future objectives: " . . . join with strong, well-respected partners in new ventures whose business phi-

142

losophy and sense of corporate citizenship corresponds with ours . . . maintain independence as a major international company, and thereby work in harmony with all segments of travel and transportation seeking the type of accommodations we provide.''

When Carlson made that statement, there was not the slightest thought in his mind that he would ever live to see anything but an independent Western International Hotels company, and at his annual meeting of Western's managers in 1969, he stated his company had no interest in any merger consideration.

One year later Western became a subsidiary of UAL, Inc., and a corporate partner of United Airlines. "The House of Friendship" and "The Friendly Skies" were now neighbors under the same roof.

Why? When Carlson had said Western had no interest in a merger, he had no idea that United was or would ever be thinking about such an arrangement. When he learned that was indeed the case, he and his associates saw the remarkable possibilities of an affiliation with United. Both companies were in essentially the same business of serving travelers. Both companies complemented each other quite well in the United States, and to some extent in Canada. Both companies saw the same potential growth in business and personal travel. Both companies had the same business philosophies, the same dedication to quality of service, the same sense of responsibility to customers, employees, and shareholders.

So the merger negotiations got under way, and in March, 1970, the directors of UAL, Inc. and Western International Hotels approved in principle a merger between the two companies with an exchange of stock on the basis of 1.3 shares of a UAL convertible preferred stock for each share of Western International.

At a special UAL, Inc. stockholders' meeting on July 30, 1970, the WIH merger was approved as it had been by WIH stockholders. The union was legally consummated.

In the final result, the two statements Carlson made in his 1969 shareholder report to all intents and purposes proved to be correct after all:

"... to maintain independence as a major international company and to work in harmony with all segments of travel and transportation. ..."

Western International Hotels would continue as an autonomous and wholly-owned subsidiary of UAL, Inc., with management and headquarters remaining in Seattle. Of course it would work closely with United Airlines as "partners in travel," but it would work with other airlines and other segments of travel, as United would work effectively with other hotels and hotel systems.

"... to join with strong, well-respected partners in new ventures whose business philosophy and sense of corporate citizenship corresponds with ours. ..."

That statement stands for itself.

Three years after its merger with UAL, Inc., Western was operating or was affiliated with almost 20,000 hotel rooms in 12 countries throughout the world, and in the remainder of the seventies planned to add 15,000 more new guest rooms, one of the largest complements of quality guest rooms in the hotel industry.

In return, it would give up its chairman and chief executive to UAL, Inc., and United Airlines; and while that was never contemplated when the merger was negotiated, it turned out to be the most dramatic and significant result of the entire deal.

The headwinds of change

I n the first four years of George Keck's term as chief executive officer, United recorded a tremendous growth, from a 1966 volume of $926 million to a 1969 gross of $1.5 billion.

In the fourth Keck year, UAL, Inc. recorded a net profit of $47.7 million; United Airlines earned $44.7 million of that total, one of the best years in its history.

In the fifth Keck year, UAL, Inc. sustained a net loss of $41 million; United Airlines alone lost $46 million—biggest in its history—and Keck was ousted from his job.

What had gone wrong? United had faced financial setbacks from time to time as it soared up the growth curve. When they happened, management acted to correct the causes and to improve profitability, and went about its business. Why, then, this sudden and drastic action? For one thing, the arithmetic had gotten bigger and bigger, and a $41 million loss on a gross of $1.5 billion was cause for serious alarm. But this was not the only reason for a major change in management. There were contributing factors which combined to make the outcome inevitable:

1. A three-way industry-wide crunch—higher costs, lower fares, and a flattened market—that had its full impact in 1970.

2. The brutalizing effect upon United of what some observers call the worst route decision in the history of the CAB—the infamous Transpacific Case.

3. The arrival on the airlines' doorstep of a premature and outsized new addition—the 747.

4. The financial collapse of the biggest railroad in the world.

5. A progressive deterioration of communication between top management and outside directors.

There were other negative forces: the 737's costly crew complement issue; the refusal of the CAB to approve the 1970 transcontinental schedule capacity agreements; the late cancellation of United's long-delayed $56 million computer program and a hasty shift to an IBM system. But those five principal factors—and above all, the crucial one of inadequate, ineffective, and ultimately, no meaningful communications at all—led to Keck's removal.

Point 1—the devastating combination of spiraling costs, lowering rates, and a leveling market—affected all airlines, and in TWA and Pan American, American and Eastern, the ultimate result would be essentially the same as in United—top management upheaval, replacement of chief executive officers in most cases, infusion of new senior officers from the outside.

In United's case the removal of Keck in itself was shocking; equally so was the action of the UAL directors in going outside for a new chief executive officer when the company was presumably deep in management bench strength. As the cold winds of change swept across the industry, it appeared that the second generation of top airline management—trained from within and brought up through evolutionary promotions, perhaps more specialist than generalist oriented—could not cope with the monumental financial leverages involved. Historic actions which had successfully dealt with past crises no longer worked because the arithmetic had grown out of hand. With huge new equipment debts to be serviced, with payroll dollars amounting to many hundreds of millions annually, big airlines could no longer afford to get very far into the red. This was especially so when outside directors exercised their responsibility to the stockholders they represent; UAL's directors were acutely conscious of the Penn Central disaster, and their responsibility to the shareholders.

So the directors accepted the proposal advanced by Executive Committee Chairman Thomas Gleed, with Gardner Cowles's concurrence, that Keck be moved out of the driver's seat and into the chairmanship, and that a new chief executive officer be brought in from the outside. The fact that Keck departed from the scenario and brought about his exit from United was a momentarily embarrassing complication; the result was the same.

The UAL directors selected one of their membership to become president and chief executive officer of both UAL, Inc., and United Airlines. Edward E. Carlson accepted their mandate to accomplish a turnaround—a turnaround that actually had already been started. What Carlson was mainly brought in to do was to change the company's direction itself. And that would prove to be no small job.

An objective account of the fateful December days of 1970 is not easy to construct. The episode can perhaps best be told in the words of a professional third-party observer, Rush Loving, Jr., a *Fortune* magazine editor who interviewed the principals and then reported in part in *Fortune,* March, 1972:

"George Keck is still bitter about the circumstances that surrounded his removal as chief executive officer of United Airlines on December 18, 1970. Until now he has not spoken about it publicly, partly, he says, because he did not want to bring further grief to his wife, Harriet, who died last summer. Keck charges that he was ousted by 'a kangaroo court, hastily called' by a cabal of directors who secretly plotted his overthrow.

"The fact is that United's directors, unlike the boards of some other troubled companies—most notably Penn Central—recognized that a management problem existed

147

and did something about it. They faced up to their fiduciary responsibilities and promptly replaced their president, an agonizing act for them because they all liked George Keck and did not want to hurt him. . . .

"United's 16-man board is an impressive group, including Justin Dart, chairman and president of Dart Industries, the drug and chemical combine; Charles F. Luce, chairman and chief executive of New York's Consolidated Edison Co.; and General Lauris Norstad, chairman and chief executive officer of Owens-Corning Fiberglas Corp. Two members of the executive committee were to play the key role in Keck's departure: Gardner Cowles, the tall, aristocratic chairman of Cowles Communications, and Thomas F. Gleed, a Seattle financier and a shrewd but charming deal maker whom Keck now refers to caustically as 'the poor man's Howard Hughes.' The directors insist that they were really anxious to help Keck succeed. They were all sympathetic to the problems of a chief executive officer, especially a new one, for almost every man on the board was or had been a chief executive officer himself. But almost from the first they found Keck abrupt, aloof, and unresponsive to suggestions. And relations deteriorated dramatically in 1969 when United suffered three body blows, each costing millions in profits.

"The first was the transpacific route case, in which United had a vital interest because it had been reaping as much as $14 million a year in profits from the Hawaii-Mainland run . . . When the final transpac decisions came down, and five other carriers were allowed into the Hawaiian market, United soon found itself losing $17 million a year on that route alone.

"Then there was the question of crew size on the Boeing 737's that United had bought for short-haul service. Even before the 737 was delivered, the pilots' union demanded that a flight engineer be allowed to ride in the cockpit, on a small seat behind the pilot . . . During the contract negotiations in 1968 the union insisted that the third man be written into the agreement, and United firmly refused. Finally it became obvious to everyone that the third-man issue would have to be arbitrated or else United would take a strike. 'Please let the board know what you are doing, who you are going to get as an arbitrator,' Gleed told Keck, reminding him that, if the decision went against United, it would cost more than $100 million over the lifetime of the planes. 'You've got no business taking a $100 million rap all by yourself.'

"But Keck felt there was little to tell the board, and that the union demand was so patently absurd United was bound to win. When the arbitrators, including United's appointee, chose unanimously for the three-man crew, Keck took the $100 million rap. 'I didn't think any rational, reasonable men would rule the way these arbitrators have ruled,' he said. Since then, to the directors' added unhappiness, another airline, Aloha, has *won* a similar arbitration.

"In early 1970, at the same time the 737 and the transpac problems were coming to a head, Keck had to inform the board that he was cancelling a $56 million computer contract that United had given to Sperry Rand's Univac division in 1965. The contract called for a massive, on-line reservation system that could handle such additional functions as flight planning and inventory. Supervision of the project was placed directly in Keck's office. But the computer programming proved unable to meet the requirements, and by 1969 the system was hopelessly tangled in problems. The project was running a year behind schedule, and the board had been asking Keck periodically how things were coming along. When Keck decided at last to cancel the contract and give the job to IBM, his decision came out of the blue to the board. The directors began to get the very definite impression that Keck was having trouble coming to decisions. And without question, as they saw it, he was not keeping them well enough informed.

"Keck was not aware that this chain of events had

deeply undermined the directors' confidence in him. There was a growing uneasiness in the back of their minds, although few of them voiced their misgivings at this stage, even with each other. The two exceptions were Gleed and Cowles, who by 1969 were in regular correspondence about the problems at United and Keck's shortcomings as president.

"As their disquiet grew, the airline business went into a slump in late 1969. Keck made plans to cut schedules and thereby cut back on the payroll. But as the slow-down continued into the winter, the general state of the nation's economy began to trouble Curtis Barkes, United's executive vice- president for finance. Barkes, who has since retired from that job but is still a director and a member of the UAL executive committee, is considered a financial wizard within the transportation industry. During the winter and on into the spring of 1970, he began to discuss his concern with Cowles, and then with Gleed. Barkes believed—correctly, as things have turned out—that the Nixon Administration economists, and United's in-house soothsayers, were predicting a turnaround that was unrealistically premature. And Keck was retrenching only in a limited fashion, at far too conservative a pace to overcome a long slump of any major proportion.

"Gleed and Cowles pressed Keck for deeper cost cutting at the June meeting of the executive committee, which Cowles remembers as 'a very rough meeting.' They repeated their suggestions at the July and August sessions and at the September 24 meeting of the full board, where Barkes urged his boss to come up with a definite profit plan within a month. The October directors meeting was the grimmest yet, and it was so full of bad news it ran much longer than usual. Keck reported that if the economy failed to improve, the company would probably run up a loss of $30 million for 1970. He did say that he was cutting further on schedules, and that many more workers, most of them ramp people and stewardesses, would be laid off. For the first time in 22 years, the board voted to pass up United's regular quarterly dividend, 25 cents per share.

"Edward Carlson, who had been on the board since August, spoke up for the first time at this meeting, calling for a definite schedule of cost cutting and the kind of profit plan proposed by Barkes the month before. Carlson's comments were not lost on the directors, who were well aware that the former shareholders of Western International now controlled 17 percent of UAL's equity. The remarks would also be remembered two months later when the directors began their search for a new chief executive.

"After the October meeting, Gleed, Cowles, and Keck agreed to meet again on November 17 in Cowles' office in New York. On that occasion Gleed plunged right in. 'George, when you took over from Pat, you took over a hell of a good staff,' he said. Then he listed the men who were retiring or were ill and pointed out that by Keck's own admission there was no one in the wings ready to succeed him. . . .

"The men agreed to hold an informal meeting of the board on December 14, the day before the next regular meeting, in order to discuss cost cutting and the thinness of management at United. But Cowles and Gleed were dispirited, feeling that Keck had not grasped the full import of their message. . . .

"The two men saw that they were headed for a showdown with Keck, yet they did not know whether they could carry the board. They decided to sound out the senior member, Justin Dart, an old friend, and Dart soon joined the inner circle of Gleed, Cowles, and Barkes. For the next two weeks the group debated what to do with Keck, whether to put someone in over him or to kick him upstairs. On the evening of December 7, Barkes, speaking for the group, telephoned Carlson at a hotelmen's convention in Mexico City and asked if he would agree to become chairman and chief executive of the UAL holding company. Keck would continue to run the airline, under Carlson's supervision.

"Carlson was surprised, but he was also dismayed at the increasing losses and at Keck's slowness to act. Furthermore, he felt a distinct responsibility to the Western shareholders. He had led them into a merger with a company that was now speeding downhill. If the board wanted him to be chairman, said Carlson, he would do it. Barkes relayed the good news, but as the week went by, the group began leaning toward the alternative solution of kicking Keck upstairs as chairman and bringing in an outsider to run the airline.

"What Gleed now calls 'the star-chamber proceeding' took place on the night of Sunday, December 13, at a meeting of the outside directors in the governor's suite at the Continental Plaza, Western's hotel in Chicago. Gleed played host, signing the check, and Keck was not invited. The directors talked over dinner and drinks for two and one-half hours. Gleed presented his bill of particulars against Keck's management. He told the group about the meetings he and Cowles had had with Keck, and he explained that the special board session had been set up for the next afternoon in hopes Keck could answer specific questions about his plans for cutting costs. When he had finished, Gleed asked the other directors how they felt. And to his surprise, there was no dissent. The others said they had shared the same uneasiness, but they had said nothing themselves because they had assumed the executive committee would keep matters in hand. When Gleed asked each man if he would support a resolution to move Keck to chairman and put in a new president and chief executive officer, each said he would.

"All the UAL directors gathered the next afternoon in the boardroom at United's executive offices in suburban Elk Grove, and there they discovered that Keck had prepared a surprise. He saw the challenge from Gleed and Cowles simply as a challenge to his record as chief executive. He was proud of that record, so proud that, as in the case against the three-man crew, he believed the directors would find no alternative but to give that record a vote of confidence. In that spirit, Keck cut the lights and, operating the slide projector himself, gave the board a three-and-one-half-hour lecture on his five years as president. He noted that United had enjoyed an annual revenue growth rate of 13.6 percent, surpassed among the five largest carriers only by Eastern, which had 13.7 percent. He pointed out that United's passenger traffic had grown 15.2 percent, the best in the league. He chronicled how, in some years, United had run up the biggest operating profit of any of the five carriers, and he reminded the directors that the other four lines had also been suffering losses.

"Keck suggested he would be glad to answer questions, if there were any. There were none. It was Cowles who finally broke the silence. 'George,' he said, 'if you could be excused, the directors would like to meet with themselves.' Keck looked surprised, got up and left. Then Cowles turned to Gleed. 'It's your meeting, Mr. Chairman.'

"'Gentlemen,' Gleed said, glancing around the table, 'it is obvious we have management problems. What is your pleasure?' The resolution they had prepared the night before, calling for a new chief executive, was then read, and, to ensure that each man was firmly committed, Gleed polled the board. The resolution passed unanimously. . . .

"Next day, with Keck presiding, the directors again passed—official this time—the resolution they had approved the previous afternoon. The resolution was not read aloud, and although he knew its meaning, Keck never saw it. He left without saying a word to anybody. . . .

"At the close of Monday's informal session, the directors had agreed that Dart should head a special committee to find the new president. The other members were

Barkes, Charles Luce, and Robert Stuart of Quaker Oats. The four of them met together off and on Monday night and Tuesday. On Wednesday, Dart, Gleed, Cowles, and the committee members were busy telephoning each other back and forth across the country. After reviewing the names of possible candidates, the attention of the committee turned to Gleed's old Seattle friend, Edward Carlson. By Thursday morning Dart had made up his mind, and he called Gleed to say that he and the committee were ready to recommend Carlson to the board. Dart then notified Carlson, who had to leave a board meeting of Seattle-First National Bank to take the call. Afterward, Carlson returned to the boardroom, but he was so stunned that he just sat there for the rest of the session, unable to concentrate on the business being transacted around him.

"Because the directors were flying in from all over the country just to vote Carlson in as chief executive, Friday's meeting was held late in the afternoon at O'Hare, around a scarred vinyl-topped table in a spartan conference room. Dart presented his recommendation, but then, with no warning, Keck got in his last word. Pulling out a sheaf of lined note pages, he began to read a handwritten statement that he had shown to no one except his wife. He denounced the meeting as a 'kangaroo court.' He said that if the board had come to him directly and had told him openly that it wanted to bring in a new president, he might have gone along. But this way he was the victim of a cabal, a conspiracy by a group of king makers, and he would not submit by becoming chairman. As he read the statement, Keck recalls, 'I kept thinking to myself, I came up the hard way. I can remember the end of the week when we were happy to have two dollars in the bank account, and I go back to that without all the niceties of a chauffeured car and this nice office.' Keck finished reading, put the papers back into his pocket, got up and put on his hat and overcoat.

"The directors sat there in shocked silence. As Keck

headed for the door, Justin Dart . . . tried to persuade him not to quit. 'I know you are acting emotionally, but it's not in your own interest,' he said. After hearing Dart out for two or three minutes, Keck walked out.

"Gleed and Dart restored order, and the board elected Keck chairman and Carlson president and chief executive. The pressing question now was how to dissuade Keck from quitting. The directors agreed that someone should go and talk with him, and Carlson volunteered, saying that their relationship had always been good. 'Eddie, you should do it—now!' said Dart, and the meeting broke up. Carlson went into the passenger service manager's office, and, after several tries to get Keck on the phone at his home, he went over in person.

"For more than two hours Carlson pleaded with Keck, and when he left he had the definite impression that Keck might indeed reconsider. But Keck had made up his mind once and for all. Dart tried to call him time and again the next day, and Keck refused to take the calls. Finally, Keck gave in and answered. 'I gave you my answer yesterday,' he said. Dart then enlisted the aid of Templeton Brown, a highly respected Chicago lawyer, who went to Keck's office and pleaded with him for about thirty minutes. When Brown returned home, he called Dart in Los Angeles. 'No chance. No way,' he said. Keck was resigning and that was that."[1]

As a sequel, Brown opened up conversations with Keck which led to a negotiation for payment of a substantial sum to Keck over a period of five years as a condition of his departure from United, during which period he would not become involved directly or indirectly with another airline. He remained a director of the company until the following April when his name was not placed in nomination for reelection. In all other respects his association with United had ended.

1. Rush Loving, Jr., "How A Hotelman Got the Red Out of United Air Lines," *Fortune* (March, 1972).

Keck remains convinced the factors which brought on the 1970 slump—the cost-price squeeze, the transpacific route case impact, the CAB's slowness in assisting the carriers—were not given sufficient weight by the directors. He felt the series of moves he and his associates initiated during late 1969 and 1970 to deal with the financial problem—schedule reductions and personnel layoffs, for example—were discounted as too little, too late. He says that he resisted outside director pressures to make what he felt were personnel cuts so deep they would permanently harm United, along with pressures to move out several senior officers who served on his management team and shared his corporate decisions.

Keck challenges the charge he failed to communicate with the directors. In his meetings with the executive committee as well as with the full board, he states that he conveyed "pertinent, detailed information on all matters of import that were of concern to management and the board. If the charge of a lack of communication on my part is made," Keck said, "I would have to make the counter charge that the executive committee did not listen or understand."

In retrospect and at the distance of several years, it appears that for one reason or another, ineffective communication was the core of the problem. What one person may believe to be clear communication can appear to be a confused blur to someone else. Good communication is difficult to achieve under the best circumstances, and with friction and suspicion in the picture, the outcome is usually failure.

Again in retrospect, the welfare of United Airlines was served, for the time had come when a shift in policy priorities was required, and only a positive change in the direction of the company could have achieved essential financial stability on a permanent basis. Only such a change could have steeled the organization to better survive in the harsh environment of the seventies. Only such a change could have restored the necessary confidence of the directors and shareholders in management. The change was severe, but the effect proved to be beneficial.

The basic relationship between outside directors and management had been strengthened. Management still manages under policies approved by directors, until and unless management fails to perform—and then directors move to correct or change, on behalf of the shareholders they represent. But to fulfill their responsibility, they must be properly informed about corporate affairs, and participate in policy considerations. Certainly the crucial lesson is the familiar one of the need for good communication, and the penalty for management's failure to fulfill that need. The reciprocal of this is the responsibility of the directors to make sure their communication lines to management are open, operating, and meaningful.

And so an era in United Airlines came to an end on December 21, 1970. It ended painfully and with finality.

The personal management philosophies and techniques of the first and second generations of top airline managers could no longer serve the corporate requirements of the seventies. Now the airlines—like corporations in other fields of industry—needed a management style wholly dedicated to the proposition that profits must be achieved and maximized. Without profits there will be no corporations, no capitalism, no free enterprise; there will be no employees, no shareholders. The profit objective can no longer be simply an effect; it must be the cause as well. This must be the doctrine of all business and industry in today's demanding environment. Of course, the airlines' management is basically to serve the public, but they must do so with a positive economic result.

Some older airline managers have been able to adapt to this more impersonal, relentless pattern of modern management; others have not. But the old era was gone, and United Airlines would never be the same again.

In looking elsewhere for a leader of the modern mold,

the board of directors was fortunate to choose one who could satisfy the shareholders and the financial houses, yet who could sense and fulfill the personal values of the customer relationship, and who knew intuitively and from experience as well that corporate profits in a "people" business really start from serving customers well. And in addition, it chose one who understood the indispensable roles of the employees in providing that quality of service.

In such a profit philosophy lay the road to the airlines' big new era, and the route to United's continued leadership in the years to come.

The Board of Directors of UAL, Inc., and United Airlines as it was constituted in March, 1972: (Seated, L to R) Justin Dart, Curtis Barkes, John J. Mitchell**, W. A. Patterson***, Gardner Cowles, and Charles F. Luce. (Standing, L to R) Semon E. Knudsen, C. F. McErlean*, Marvin Whitlock*, L. P. Himmelman, Richard P. Cooley, Byron J. Nichols, William M. Jenkins, Edward E. Carlson, Lauris Norstad, H. Templeton Brown, Aksel Nielsen, R. E. Bruno*, Thomas F. Gleed, Robert E. Johnson*, and Vernon Stouffer. Robert D. Stuart, Jr. not present,

*Director of United Airlines only
**Director Emeritus
***Director Emeritus and
Honorary Chairman

The soaring Seventies

W hen Edward E. Carlson was elected president and chief executive officer of UAL, Inc. and United Airlines, some people wondered what a hotel man might know about air transportation and how he could manage an airline.

Eddie Carlson likes to say that the hotel business and air transportation have a good deal in common. Hotels are concerned with housing people in bedrooms, airlines with putting people in airplane seats. Hotel people deal in bedroom nights, airlines in revenue passenger miles. Hotels are concerned with house counts or percent of room occupancy, airlines count load factors or percent of seats occupied. In both cases customers are travelers, whether for business or personal reasons. So hotels and airlines indeed have a strong common purpose—both are in the people business, and the success of any hotel or airline depends upon how well it serves its customers.

While this point was conceded by persons who questioned the selection of Carlson to head the Free World's largest airline, they still had reservations about his ability to deal with many problems unique to air transportation. Some predicted he wouldn't last a year in this pressure situation. What they didn't know was that Eddie Carlson had been an active participant in the affairs of UAL, Inc. and United Airlines before he took command, and was one of the larger single stockholders in the airline's holding company. Officially he became a part of United when

UAL, Inc. acquired Western International Hotels in July of 1970, but practically speaking he had been well acquainted with United for a much longer period of time. What they also didn't know was that Carlson was thoroughly qualified as a business leader.

As he had moved into higher management in the hotel business, two traits were greatly responsible for his success. First he exhibited a natural talent and flair for personal relations; having worked his way up from the bottom rung of the ladder, he had learned that to get things done you must motivate people and inspire them by the example of leadership. Possessing a warm, outgoing personality, he found that "getting along" with people came naturally to him, and he cultivated this as one of the important tools of management. At the same time—and sometimes in conflict with his "people-to-people" approach, he had a clear grasp of the principle of free enterprise that establishes profit as the aim of corporate life—profit for the employee, for the stockholder, as well as for management.

He perceived the value of the profit center approach, and he had applied this formula with success in Western Hotels. He saw that good managers were selected and properly trained for their responsibilities. Carlson's emphasis on profit was not mutually exclusive of the importance of good human relations, for no service business can be profitable unless it wins and retains the goodwill of customers. Western Hotels developed an enviable record for courtesy and hospitality in its field, and veteran and inexperienced travelers alike were quick to appreciate the friendly service they received. But as he encouraged this concept of service, Carlson also stressed profitability as the principal mission of his managers, and Western Hotels was conspicuous for its profitable results. As it expanded from a few to many units throughout the United States and Canada, as well as Mexico and other parts of the world, it consistently returned a profit for its shareholders.

Soon after Carlson was elected chief executive officer of UAL, Inc., and of United Airlines, its subsidiary company, he stepped aside as chairman and chief executive officer of Western International Hotels, to be succeeded by Lynn Himmelman and with Gordon Bass moving up to the presidency.

He wasted no time. From Seattle he sent advance word that he wanted a meeting of the senior officers of United Airlines in 48 hours, and he wanted them to be ready at that time with their own estimates of the ten highest priority actions facing the company.

At the end of that meeting, on the third day of his presidency, ten corporate objectives had been clearly defined, agreed to, and ranked according to priority.

His next action was to set up what he termed the "Senior Management Committee" of United Airlines. For years the company had operated with a general staff composed of the senior officers, but its weekly meetings had been oriented primarily for exchange of information rather than for policy development and direction. The new Senior Management Committee was to share in the evolution of policies as well as in the solving of major problems.

Chaired by Carlson, the "SMC" included Charles F. McErlean, executive vice-president and general manager; Robert E. Johnson, senior vice-president for marketing; Rex Bruno, senior vice-president—finance; William Dunkle, senior vice-president—flight; A. M. de Voursney, senior vice-president—economic planning; Marvin Whitlock, senior vice-president—operations; Percy Wood, senior vice-president—personnel; Brien Fennell, senior vice-president—law; George Kidera, senior medical director; and Richard Dimpfl, corporate secretary. Within a few months Johnson was elected executive vice-president, and was succeeded as senior vice-president—marketing by R. L. Mangold who was added to the committee.

Typical of Carlson's management habit, the Senior

Management Committee did its work at luncheon sessions. One advantage of this was to save time, but important in Carlson's mind was the sense of urgency that this type of business meeting would develop among the company's senior officers.

Along with urgency of action came accountability, and senior officers were made expressly accountable for policy decisions and actions that involved them. Carlson introduced one of his favorite management techniques—group policy consideration. The result would be total commitment to whatever action was determined; second-guessing stopped at that point.

Another move by the new president was an attack on the communication gap that existed in United Airlines, as it does in most business organizations when busy executives don't take the time to tell others what they are doing. Applying the acronym "NETMA" which he had coined in Western Hotels—*Nobody Ever Tells Me Anything*—Carlson went after United's communication gap with diligence. For a while everybody began telling each other everything, but as the SMC settled down and became accustomed to the new order, hard information about specific policies and problems began to be freely exchanged and trivial information and gossip were forgotten.

Thus Carlson accomplished another immediate objective—to get the top management officers working as a well-informed team, not as a group of individuals. The results were remarkable—remarkable to everyone except Carlson, for he encountered the first of some major frustrations he was to experience. He was dismayed by the slowness with which, in his eyes, it took to get something done. Admittedly United Airlines was a different organization from Western Hotels, far larger and geographically broader. Its chain of communication was more extended and involved more organizational steps. Recognizing all this, Carlson still felt that it took too long to get something done. Part of the problem seemed to be resistance to change, part a habitual deliberateness of action, part plain inertia. Whatever the causes, Carlson assigned to himself the priority of speeding up the action processes of the company.

He told the employees of United Airlines, "The directors of this company have charged me with the task of returning United to the profitability it should and must achieve." He went on to say to the Senior Management Committee, "This is a responsibility you share with me, and you and I cannot fulfill it alone. It will require the actions of everybody in United Airlines." Quite naturally this became the first of the ten goals and objectives set forth to chart the corporation's new course.

The plant size of an airline cannot be quickly reduced as can the production line of a factory. Nonetheless, prompt and energetic steps were taken to bring about a further reduction in the scope of United Airlines's operations, primarily by cutting back on schedule frequencies. Carlson instinctively felt that every schedule United Airlines operated—in effect, every product unit United Airlines "manufactured"—should be profitable. He listened to the persuasive arguments that market share required some unprofitable schedules to be operated with those that were profitable, but he found himself unable to accept this kind of argument. So considerable schedule mileage in highly competitive markets was lopped off unilaterally long before industry agreements among several carriers were negotiated with the blessing of the Civil Aeronautics Board. He listened to the explanation that the certificate under which the company operated by authority of the Civil Aeronautics Board resulted in some schedules being operated at a loss into small markets, but he felt there was no reason why such schedules could not be reduced to a necessary minimum. He heard the argument that some schedules are developmental in nature, over new routes or routes that had not been previously served, and that time was required to build such schedules into profitability. This kind of a business risk he understood, but he insisted that there be a finite limit to the period of development, and this, too, resulted in some schedule reduction. All in all the cutbacks which went into effect early in 1971 represented a $30 million step toward the black for the year, a big chunk of the necessary make-up total.

Other pruning came in smaller amounts: the advertising budget; more conservative cruise control of schedule flights to save kerosene; food service where some frills were dropped without interfering with the basic quality of the service to the customer.

Carlson found that the airline business is like the hotel business in that both are labor intensive. About 45 percent of United's expense dollar went to wages and salaries, and this meant an estimated payroll in 1971 of over $750 million. Here was where drastic action would be required. Carlson asked for and received commitment from the Senior Management Committee for a major reduction in personnel. This was to come slowly but surely, and in the end a reduction of about 10 percent from the planned number of employees at peak 1971 was realized. This was a painful approach, for it meant the furloughing of many able, loyal, and dedicated personnel —pilots, stewardesses, ground employees of all types; and yet the alternative would be continued operation in the red, leading to the loss of many more jobs.

Such steps were to bring the company within $5 million of its goal of at least breakeven in 1971. While the objective of return to profitability was not accomplished in Carlson's first year, the result did represent a great improvement over the $41 million lost in 1970.

But these were fire-fighting emergency measures, and while successful, they were only preliminary to the fundamental change of direction Carlson was planning. His next move was to restructure the organization, which was so large and layered with different management levels, it was slow to respond to new decisions and it was not flexible enough to meet promptly the changing circumstances that faced the airline. Furthermore, the matter of achieving profit was more often one of effect rather than cause. What Carlson now wanted was the profit center concept. Neither United nor any other large airline lends itself to the application of the orthodox profit center technique; however, he was not backed off by this fact, but instead said, "Let's get a piece of it, let's take what we can get." Reorganization became a top long-term priority in the company. "Long term" in Carlson's vocabulary meant no more than a year; before the year was out, major changes had been initiated.

The result was a decentralization of the operating organization into three divisions—Eastern, Central, and Western. It was a basic objective that authority for day-to-day operating decisions be pushed out into the field and down through organization levels as far as possible. Parallel with this was the concept that responsibility for achieving profit would be vested in the field operating management to the greatest possible extent.

Such a drastic change in organizational structure could not be accomplished as quickly as Carlson would have liked to see, but before the end of the year the divisions were structured, the senior officers selected, and their staffs completed. By the first of the next year the three operating divisions had been established, and were in fact running the day-to-day operation of the airline under Charles McErlean, who as executive vice-president and chief operating officer, reported directly to Carlson, and on whom Carlson relied heavily as his closest business associate.

The three operating divisions were the Eastern, headed by Senior Vice-president Percy Wood; the Central under the direction of R. L. Mangold; and the Western, managed by Ralph Glasson (who came to the line from a vice-presidency in the maintenance base and after the Western Division was established and operating, returned to that post and was succeeded by James Hartigan). Support divisions were set up at headquarters for marketing, cost control, personnel, maintenance, and flight, also reporting to McErlean.

To formalize the functioning of the operational organization, an Operations Management Committee was established, chaired by McErlean, and composed of the three divisional operating officers, as well as the heads of the various other divisions, such as food service and maintenance.

The conduct of corporate affairs—the fixing of corporate policies—the administration of the company's basic objectives, and profit goals—were of course another matter. The corporate elements were reorganized to provide these major divisions: External Affairs directed by Executive Vice-president Johnson (to be succeeded upon his retirement in 1972 by Senior Vice-president Mechlin Moore), Corporate Planning headed by Senior Vice-president de Voursney, and Finance under Senior Vice-president Bruno. To insure appropriate guidance of the corporation, Carlson set up a Corporate Policy Committee composed of Charles McErlean and the other senior corporate officers and chaired by himself. The CPC, as it was identified, met weekly—and often more frequently—to consider all policy matters and to make policy decisions, subject where appropriate to the approval of the corporate board of directors. Thus the CPC and OMC fulfilled Carlson's desire for committee conduct of policy matters and day-to-day operating routine.

As he reworked the structure of the organization and reoriented it to the profit goal, he took stock of the company's responsibilities to others, and to their needs. Here are his words on that subject:

"Management must deal fairly with the interests of three groups of partners—customers, employees and shareholders.

"First, the customers. What do they want? They want to fly or ship goods in aircraft that represent the latest in comfort and technology—scheduled at times that fit their plans. They want the maximum amount of service and in-flight amenities. And in addition, they want these things at the lowest possible price. In short, they want all they can get.

"Second, employees. When we analyze their desires —whether management or nonmanagement—we find they want good working conditions, good pay, adequate benefits for themselves and their families, and, I quickly learned, good pass privileges. In short, all they can get.

"Third, the shareholders. When they come into the market to invest in common stocks, they're interested in a company that has a reasonably consistent dividend record; a company that has sustained growth over a period of years with appreciation in the value of its shares; a company that has liquidity. In other words, the shareholders want all they can get.

"Now the challenge to business is to keep constant and proper balance among these three sensitive groups. If a priority must be established, it must rest with customers. Without their support, we don't need employees, and shareholders will disappear rapidly.

"In air transportation the fine tuning is further complicated by a fourth partner—the government. Ours is a regulated industry. What does government want? It wants the finest privately owned and operated air transport system in the world. It wants the lowest possible rates for military movements, material, and the shipment of mail. It wants growth in tax revenues. In short, government wants all it can get."

Carlson came to United to find a long history of chilly relations with the Civil Aeronautics Board, punctuated occasionally by icy criticism of that agency. United had gained the reputation at the Board of being against it, and of opposing many things the Board did or proposed doing. To Carlson this seemed to be contrary to good business judgment and practice. He looked on the government as a partner, and he felt the government should be so treated. One of his first actions was to adopt the philosophy that the company would support rather than oppose the Civil Aeronautics Board, and that he recognized the need for understanding and cooperation. He did not intend to roll over when the Board might take some action contrary to United's and the industry's best interests, but he did intend to get along with the Board.

Both in his public statements and in his company policy, he consistently reflected this philosophy, so much so that CAB Chairman Secor Browne at one point characterized the advent of Carlson as United president as a "breath of fresh air in the industry."

While both parties have maintained this spirit of respect and understanding, growing disillusionment developed when Carlson realized that no matter what the intention of the principals, there has been and can continue to be a natural difference of philosophy between the government agency and the scheduled carriers. This difference expresses itself, for example, in the government regulation of airline fares to provide the lowest possible fare to the public, often to the financial detriment of the carriers. The Board is inclined to view itself in the light of public defender, and while giving lip service to its responsibility for maintaining a sound and financially strong airline industry, CAB pressure to hold airline fares down despite continually rising costs had so weakened the industry's financial strength that Carlson could see the threat of nationalization as a possible result.

Toward the end of 1972, United's president focused attention on the problem in a major address before the National Association of Manufacturers, commenting:

"The airline problems which surfaced in 1970 have continued with great intensity. The airlines have been caught between the pincers of Government regulation . . . and extreme cost inflation, with a rate of inflation higher than the national average. . . .

"The Government must recognize that the financial condition of the industry influences the national economy. . . .

"The airlines need investor confidence. Obtaining capital has become increasingly difficult. By 1980, the U.S. airlines will carry 320 million passengers annually, about double today's yearly rate, and capital requirements to meet this expansion are estimated to approach $30 billion. But if the airlines continue to follow a roller-coaster pattern of profit and loss, additional financing will be even more difficult.

"When an essential industry such as air transportation reaches the point where it cannot obtain necessary capital requirements, the remaining step is nationalization in one form or another. The traditions in our country are solidly opposed to nationalization, but should a critical situation develop, the Federal Government could not permit airlines to close their doors, and it is only reasonable that nationalization would be suggested as an answer.

"Reasonable profits would go a long way to eliminate financing problems."

In discussing this problem, Carlson emphasized that the industry and the government shared responsibility for stabilizing the industry's economic future. The airlines were working diligently to achieve and to maintain effective cost management, and the government would necessarily have to permit realistic pricing. Carlson concluded:

"Despite its great accomplishments, the airline system is vulnerable, and its survival will depend on the collective wisdom of airline management, and our regulators and others in Government who share responsibility for what is today the finest air transport system in the world. The threats of possible change are there—they should be recognized and action initiated while there is still time."

A hopeful response to Carlson's observations came in early 1973, when the then newly appointed chairman of the Civil Aeronautics Board, Robert Timm, proclaimed the economic stability of the industry to be the number one priority of the Board. For many years the Board had maintained, after exhaustively examining the matter, that trunk airlines were entitled to a 10.25 percent rate of return upon investment, but in only two years had the trunk industry as a whole been able to approximate this official target. In 1972 it found the appropriate rate of return should be 12 percent. Chairman Timm stated Board policy should foster realization of that goal. The critical financial problems of the industry would be solved should that goal be attained.

But Carlson did not allow his frustration with government to obscure the fact that the future welfare of the company depended mainly on itself, and he let nothing stand in the path of his progress toward redirection of United. He redoubled his efforts to increase a sense of urgency among associates, and to improve follow-through. (A favorite remark during his initial days with United was "the numbers are big and the clock is running.") He had found in United, as in many organizations, a gap between deciding to do something and then getting it done. He hammered away upon accountability and follow-through. He considered meetings that dealt with problems and solutions without recording action assignments and completion dates to be "bull sessions." He saw no reason why things could not be accomplished promptly, and in his mind "only the impossible" could be expected to take a little longer. He was distressed by waste of resources: waste of time, waste of manpower, waste of physical assets. He tended to look on each dollar of capital expenditure and operating expense as he would a dollar of his own, and he wanted to make sure that full value was received for any expense.

He was suspicious of excess staff manpower. He was wary of what he liked to call "Josefinas"—superfluous personnel whom managers were reluctant to drop. The name "Josefina" came from a celebrated incident in Western Hotels' history when a manager orchestrated the transfer of an accountant named Josefina, whom he highly touted to a fellow manager seeking such an employee; later the manager who inherited Josefina found

174

that she was completely incompetent.

Carlson prodded, pried, and pushed United's managers to ferret out "Josefinas" and bring about greater productivity. Although keenly aware of the importance of good personnel relationships, Carlson recognized that one road to improved profit was leaning out the organization. He knew this was distasteful to many, but organizations do develop "fat" in prosperous times, and leaning out becomes necessary whether the ink is black or red.When persuasion and suggestion did not work, arbitrary steps toward reduction in the size of the organization were required, and Carlson took them, unpalatable though this course was for everyone.

In the peak summer period of 1970 there were 52,000 employees on the payroll of United Airlines. By contrast in the peak summer period of 1972 there were 49,000 employees in United Airlines, and those 49,000 personnel operated schedules which carried 25 percent more passengers than in the peak two years before. Rigid manpower control was the single most important factor in turning United around from loss to profit. United's managers learned this lesson, a lesson that had to be practiced day in and day out, year in and year out.

Carlson's philosophy of management went beyond working with the CPC and SMC. He realized that NETMA pervaded the entire organization, and it worked both ways—communication down and communication up. He wanted to meet and to talk with everyone in the company, and while he couldn't quite accomplish that objective, he did a great deal in his first year when he traveled 187,000 miles across the airline. He talked with groups of employees: stewardesses, pilots, salesmen, reservations agents, mechanics, cooks, office clerks. He talked with thousands more on the airplanes, at the stations and offices. He listened to what they had to say, he knew what was on their minds, he knew what worried them, and he learned what ideas they had to improve the company. But he wanted the other officers of the company to get the message, so he brought in groups of managers at one time and nonmanagement employees at another for day-long sessions in which they had the opportunity to talk directly with senior officers, telling what was on their minds and what they wanted to suggest. This proved to be an excellent way of getting the employee story directly to top management, and it became a regular part of United's management program.

He created an annual President's Conference, attended by all key managers from across the system. This was not too different in concept from the "Flight Plan" annual management meetings conducted through the Patterson years, and a more limited management program carried out by Keck. It did bring Carlson face to face with United's management team at the outset, and it was to become an integral part of Carlson's communication system to fight "NETMA."

In the course of his probing, Carlson discovered a communication bottleneck in middle management where information coming down from policy levels dried up and where information coming from nonmanagement employees to the higher levels was blocked. Here was a primary cause of "NETMA," and so attention was focused on the need for better communications up and down the line of the entire organization. This brought about several new media of communication with first-line supervisors as well as line employees. Slowly but surely communication was improved and slowly but surely "NETMA" was being reduced.

Having overhauled the organization, Carlson felt such a drastic change should have the check and balance of an outside audit. Over the years he had developed confidence in the consultant firm of Cresap, McCormick and Paget, and he sought their advice and counsel. The consultants reviewed the new organization, and found it well conceived and well executed. It fulfilled the modern requirement for flexibility of organizational structure and for decentralization of the operating routines. It protected the requirement that, regardless of its geography or size, a corporation must have a central policy direction and a consistent policy voice, and the corporation likewise must have top financial guidance. Paget found a problem in the absence of any corporate marketing responsibility as a result of the divisionalization of the operating functions. Carlson corrected this with the reestablishment at the corporate level of a top marketing office. The position of executive vice-president—marketing was filled by Rob Mangold, brought back from the Central Division to establish this division.

Carlson split off food service from the operational organization and set it up as a separate profit center. In the big hotel business he had been deeply involved with restaurants. United's meal and beverage bill for 1971 was forecasted to be about $70 million. The company ranked among the first 25 largest restaurant chains and among the largest liquor dispensers in the United States. Carlson wanted to make sure United's food and beverage service was being operated with maximum efficiency, and that plans were being made to capitalize on the expansion opportunities for selling food outside the airline itself.

With Western, Carlson had developed an admiration for Vic Bergeron, better known as Trader Vic, who operated a chain of successful and popular restaurants. It occurred to Carlson early in his regime that bringing Trader Vic into the United food service would be a good move, and he invited Bergeron to United's headquarters, had him look over the food operation, meet the chefs and the managers of the department, and then he negotiated an agreement to establish Trader Vic service. Mercurial by temperament, Bergeron had immediate problems with United's personnel and vice versa, but after some painful adjustments, Trader Vic service was initiated and it captured much public attention and customer attraction.

Meantime, Carlson had been looking for a young, aggressive profit-oriented manager who could run the food service department to his satisfaction. He found him in the person of Dick Ferris, a bright, driving, successful manager in the Western Hotels chain, and Ferris was named to head United's Food Service Division, reporting directly to Carlson. Ferris guided the new division enthusiastically yet carefully along its new road, and demonstrated his outstanding managerial skills.

Subsequently, Carlson brought Percy Wood, Eastern Division general manager, into the executive offices where his long background at the engineering and maintenance base was put to good use in a new post of group vice-president for a number of operational functions including the maintenance base. To take over the vital Eastern Division in the hotly competitive Atlantic Coast market places, Mangold was moved to New York. His direction of marketing was assumed by Ferris, as group vice-president of marketing functions including system marketing, in-flight and ground services, along with the food division.

One of Carlson's self-contradictions is his impatience with torrents of reports and other paper he finds cascading throughout United, yet he himself is so addicted to communication that on occasion his office becomes a sort of geyser spewing out awesome amounts of committee reports and statistical attachments. In Carlson's mind the key is not how much paper is there, but what's on the paper. One of his early hangups with United was the sea of financial statistics so deep that by the time he could find out why the bottom line was red, white, or black, the next month's river of accounting data began to empty into its own sea. What Carlson wanted was a simplified "early warning" system of financial data that would provide him the meaty information and profit trends which could be changed before instead of after the fact, if changes were indicated. He brought in John Olsson, chief financial officer in the U.S. Department of Transportation, to head a combined team of United and Arthur Andersen accounting people to simplify and to refine the company's business informational system, and to further refine the profit center application. This program resulted in multiplying individual profit centers.

Carlson continued to apply his philosophy of cross-fertilizing United's internal management when he placed Monte Lazarus, formerly administrative assistant to the CAB chairman, as head of United's Washington office which proved to be a good move, and Dwight Chapin, former presidential appointments secretary at the White House, as market planning director, which proved otherwise. At the beginning of 1974, Carlson had several officers who had come in from the outside: Mechlin Moore, Dick Ferris, James Kent (a Western Hotel official who had succeeded Ferris in charge of United's food services) and Lazarus, along with Olsson. He was not discarding the traditional United philosophy of promotion from within, but he knew that a change in corporate direction meant a new management viewpoint, and to satisfy that need he felt it necessary to bring outside men in to serve on his team.

In his quest for improvements and new ideas, Carlson gave some thought to United's public face. It appeared to be good—reflecting strength, character, competence, and dignity and other desirable attributes of a corporate physiognomy. But there did seem to be a staid, slightly wrinkled appearance when one looked at it closely. So Carlson decided to try a little face-lifting, but nothing too drastic.

For decades, the interior of United's planes had been conservative; subdued colors and solid textures had been favored to create an unobtrusive yet reassuring environment for the passengers. Carlson decided to start with the cabin decor and he introduced bright, challenging Thai silk into cabin upholstery and wall spaces. After a brief, startled interval this change was well accepted by all concerned. Then Carlson moved into a more visible— and much more sensitive—aspect of corporate imagery, the exterior of the aircraft.

For years United's Mainliners had worn red, white, and blue stripes, and had carried a version of a shield as the official emblem. When a new 1974 paint scheme emerged with striping in blue, red and orange (orange?!?) and a brand new emblem, there were immediate protests and wounded laments for the missing red, white, and blue, and the shield (until someone pointed out the shield hadn't appeared on a United plane for years). In this process Carlson achieved a partial corporate name change—from "United Air Lines" to "United Airlines" (as used throughout this book).

So the smart, contemporary look of United's planes now phasing into its fleet is helping to add a confident, fresh appearance to United's public image and it reflects the dynamism of its leader.

In three fast-moving years of Carlson's presidency he had accomplished a major reorganization of the world's largest airline, and he had reversed its financial trend. The critics who had said a hotel man couldn't run an airline were silenced; the industry experts who said the divisional concept wouldn't work had been proven wrong.

Now Carlson could turn his attention to long-range planning, and he did so with enthusiasm. How could United become and remain an airline consistently earning 12 percent on its capital base? What should United's fleet composition be in five years, or ten, or fifteen? By October, 1973, he had many of the answers from United's economic planners, and he presented a favorable five-year profit plan and an encouraging long-range fleet plan to his board of directors.

Two months later the airline industry had encountered one of the catastrophic situations which occasionally occur to cause a major upheaval.

This was the energy crisis, and it confronted Carlson and his management team with what looked for a time as the biggest problem they had yet encountered.

Down through its 50 years, the airline business has

usually been in a state of flux, and about the only constant has been the continual process of change.

The year 1973 proved to be no exception. Toward the close of a period of steady growth and improving profitability for United, the Middle East oil-producing sheikdoms forced a growing world energy shortage into an abrupt crunch for U.S. airlines. Almost overnight 1974 plans and projections became obsolete and long-term planning gave way to short-term improvisation. The sudden curtailment of kerosene supplies caused large-scale schedule cutbacks, massive personnel layoffs, lowered airplane utilization (and aircraft mothballing by some carriers), and forecasts of a temporary period of zero air market growth.

In the case of United, Carlson found that his five-year profit plan and long-range equipment program, carefully honed by corporate economists and unfolded to his board of directors, had to be temporarily shelved.

Beyond the immediate effects were the future impacts. How long would the problem exist? If fuel supplies were limited for even a few years, what would be the effect upon market growth and the carrier's ability to serve it? Would temporary personnel furloughs become permanent? How long might be the period when no new aircraft would be needed?

One phase of United's operations illustrated the effect of limitations on fuel. Prior industry schedule reductions —designated as "capacity reductions"—had originally received reluctant government approval. Now the administration praised them as responsive to the energy shortage and urged the airlines to extend this practice. But what effect would this have in years to come? Would U.S. carriers become in effect a cartel permanently fixing schedule offerings among themselves? Hardly, yet some in Congress saw the opportunity to give the CAB control of airline scheduling and unsuccessfully tried to enact such legislation. The CAB already had the power to regulate routes and rates, and adding regulation of schedules would give it practical control of airline management. The legislative proposal was withdrawn, and although the CAB disclaimed any desire to pursue the subject, the possible threat remained.

Many observers of the energy situation thought airlines would improve profits through schedule cutbacks and commensurately higher load factors, but they had failed to take into account the impact of rapidly escalating kerosene costs, which in some cases more than offset capacity economies. Carlson said:

"We alone can't solve the energy situation, but there are things we can and will do to manage our own business in the face of it. There will have to be changes in life style. While the oil shortage is real, the public refuses to believe it. We must live with that public, and serve it well, even though schedule frequency must be reduced. We must establish our credibility with our public, and produce a quality of service which will maintain consumer confidence."

Some other carriers were encountering severe financial headwinds when the energy shortage struck; United had regained a strong financial base. It could deal with this crisis from a position of strength, and it did so.

It is to Carlson's great credit that United had such renewed financial strength. He says it was a team accomplishment, and it was all of that. But it required his determined, unflagging leadership to achieve the result.

Carlson took over at the close of 1970, a year when UAL, Inc.'s losses totaled $41 million. Here is the UAL, Inc. box score for the following three years:

1971—A loss of $5 million
1972—A profit of $20 million
1973—A profit of $51 million

Carlson's real goal is "to make United the industry leader in effective profit ratios and the leader in earnings." He will never rest until he sees that goal attained: not just the largest, not just the best, but the most profitable airline in the world. As a first long step toward that

182

objective, he plans to reach and maintain the 12 percent return on investment cited as fair and reasonable by the CAB.

Eddie Carlson is determined to take that epochal step, and as the old Post Office saying goes, "Neither rain nor snow nor gloom of night,"—nor kerosene shortage for that matter—is apt to stay him from completing that self-appointed round.

Chapter 18

The future United

Approaching the close of its first half-century, United Airlines had grown from infancy to the world's largest transportation system.

When Pat Patterson became United's president, the company's dimensions seemed large—a few thousand miles of airways, 1,600 employees, 70 airplanes, annual sales of $7 million. Imaginative and positive as he was, it would have been quite difficult for Patterson to have conceived the spectacular expansion through which he was to lead the company during the next three-and-one-half decades. The generation of the thirties was too firmly rooted in the ground for anyone to envision the tremendous revolution the airplane would cause in the nation's economic, social, political, and military future.

When Eddie Carlson became United's president, the company's dimensions were large indeed—25,000 miles of airways, 51,700 employees, 375 airplanes, annual sales of $1.6 billion.

Like Patterson, Carlson is imaginative and positive. By now the air transport industry had matured, and the generation of the seventies was committed to the air, so it was easier for him to foresee the growth toward which he could lead United.

By 1980, United could be twice its 1972 size. Its fleet may not be much greater in units, but the 1980 airplanes will have many more seats and larger cargo compartments, so 1980 revenues could reach $4 billion.

More difficult than visualizing future dimensions is the task of foreseeing the changes which will be required to achieve that growth, for it will not occur automatically.

There are some signposts to mark the way to the future; here are eight such indicators which can give a reasonable approximation of the future United.

1. Its Future Mission.

The surest factor in United's future is its essentiality to the nation. The United States is totally dependent upon its airline industry as the major system of intercity common carrier passenger transport. The national economy, along with the national defense, is irrevocably committed to a strong air transport system. There is no alternative, no known replacement. The nation's welfare and its further development depend upon the airlines. This is United's greatest strength for the future—although conceivably this could prove to be a long-term liability in the unlikely form of nationalization.

As the population of the United States expands, as its business and industry grow correspondingly, as family incomes increase, and as leisure time becomes more abundant, so will United's passenger volumes gain substantially in the longer term, and become twice the 1970 base. Group and other tour business will expand, and further stimulate the predominance of pleasure travel in the market mix. United's long alertness to the charter market, which has enabled it to carry half of all scheduled airline charter traffic, will pay off in future growth.

Cargo should shed its second-cousin status in the next decade. While air freight has been alternately praised and damned, the fact is scheduled airlines are now dependent upon air cargo for survival. Currently $200 million of United's annual revenues come from mail and freight, and spell the difference between profit and loss. In a future period unconstrained by energy sources, cargo will play an increasingly important role in United.

But such growth will not just happen—forecasts are easy to project, hard to fulfill. So Carlson has increased emphasis upon corporate marketing, particularly the long-range corporate aspects. While the operating divisions are charged with transforming forecasts into real figures, corporate marketing has the task of guiding them in the right directions by insuring quality of service and the most effective ways of pricing, advertising, and merchandising that service. This is no small task, for each of United's three divisions is larger than a number of trunk airlines, and while each has its unique geography and differing market problems, all are dependent upon long-range schedules crossing division lines. There is a constant need to present a single image and standard of service to the customer who thinks of United Airlines not as three divisions, but as a single unified service. Carlson grouped the marketing functions into one major planning organization, as he had similarly grouped the operational support functions into another organizational element.

Further diversification of UAL, Inc., will bring more partners for United. To quote Carlson: "Future acquisitions should fit within the same 'mix' as United and WIH; it seems more logical to stay with the types of companies where UAL, Inc. has some opportunity of making a contribution either in experience or in services."

Without formal diversification into subsidiaries, United Airlines itself is continuing to develop substantial and profitable services to outside customers, mainly airlines, in such fields as maintenance and catering.

But in the future, as in the past and at present, United Airlines' principal mission will be the safe, comfortable, and profitable transportation of more and more passengers through its friendly skies. If properly fulfilled, that mission will insure the company's long-term future.

2. Its Future Size.

Before going to the question, "How big will United be in 1980?" consider these facts:

In 1961, United employed 28,000 people who produced 12.5 billion seat miles, 7.3 billion RPMs, and 100 million freight-ton miles. Gross revenues were $500 million and net profit after taxes $4 million.

Compare 1970 with 1961: United employed 52,000 people (+90 percent), who produced 48 billion seat miles (+400 percent), 25 billion RPMs (+350 percent), and 545 million freight-ton miles (+545 percent). Gross revenues were $1.5 billion (+300 percent) and net loss $41 million.

Compare 1973 with 1970: United employed 48,000 people (−7 percent), who produced 52 billion seat miles (+7 percent), 29 billion RPMs (+16 percent), and 650 million freight-ton miles (+19 percent). Gross revenues exceeded $2 billion (+30 percent) and the $41 million loss had been changed to a $51 million profit.

Those comparisons prove forecasting future size can be a dicey situation, but these 1980 dimensions appear feasible:

Volume—50 billion Revenue Passenger Miles
Volume—1.5 billion Freight-Ton Miles
Sales—$4 Billion
Fleet Size—400 Aircraft
Personnel—60,000

The future United will probably operate with the same type of organization as today, for the reorganization established in 1972 has appeared to flourish.

Here is how Carlson views the future organization:

"The divisional concept with strong individual leadership, geared to a profit center philosophy and recognizing that United Airlines must operate as a unified transportation system and speak with one voice, has achieved sufficient momentum to have us believe that this is a very effective management tool. Through the years, the organization chart must be adjusted to meet different conditions and this is as it should be. Conceivably, 10 years from now there could be a swing toward centralization. Each senior management group, charged with the responsibilities of operating any company, must determine what is the most effective management style for its needs at that time to maintain a satisfactory profit picture, aggressive marketing, stability of employment, dividends for shareholders and, hopefully, appreciated values of its stock.

"The relationship between the Corporate Policy Committee and the Operations Management Committee effectively separates corporate policy and day-to-day operating responsibility. The Corporate Policy Committee has applied the discipline to make difficult decisions promptly, to identify people responsible for the implementation of those decisions and hold them responsible for prompt follow through. The Operations Management Committee has been effective in handling the day-to-day operations of the airline. Most of us see no further divisions, but probably a consistent tuning of the organization, both as to make-up of personnel and of management functions from year to year. Suffice to say, I see no major changes, but probably minor ones from time to time."

When Carlson refers to "tuning personnel and management functions," he is reflecting his opinion that generalists, rather than specialists, make better top managers, a philosophy he practices with care but with determination.

Perhaps the bigger changes to come in United's future organization will not be in structure, but in the management of the structure—"who," not "what."

3. Its Future Fleet.

For the next decade or so, there is no new type airplane in United's future. Its fleet composition will consist of DC-10's, 747's, 727's, DC-8's, and 737's, in about that order of priority; as time goes by DC-8's and 737's should be phased out.

In the postwar years, United's DC-6's were followed in short order by the DC-7's, and next the DC-8's were quickly joined by 720's, Caravelles, 727's, and 737's. Then came the wide-bodied 747's and DC-10's. In 1969, United had $2.3 billion invested in aircraft, had indebtedness amounting to $891 million, and had achieved a debt-equity ratio that reached 64/36 by 1971.

Airplanes that had long, useful service lives were obsoleted by newer, faster and generally costlier types, while their operators were ending up in the financial custody of banks and insurance companies. Now there appears to be a future period of fleet stability.

As far as an SST may be concerned, only nine Concordes have been committed, these by the British and French airlines; at this writing, production of a total of 16 units has been authorized. There are those who argue that the speed of the SST will force international competitors to follow suit when Concorde service finally commences. But two factors have at least temporarily shelved any U.S. purchase of Concordes:

No U.S. airline can now afford or wants to finance an airplane that costs around $50 million apiece and carries 100 or so passengers at a high, but not yet precisely known, operating cost.

The sonic boom characteristic of the SST is such that the FAA will not permit its supersonic flight across the Continental United States.

A new factor has now entered the SST prospect—the matter of energy. Airlines will not be eager to operate an airplane that has only one-third as many seats and consumes as much or more fuel than the present wide-bodied subsonic aircraft. Engineers have calculated that it requires about 45 gallons of fuel per passenger to operate a fully loaded 747 between New York and London but about 185 gallons per passenger in a Concorde.

In time, SST development may overcome the problems of noise and economics, and there doubtless will come big and relatively quiet supersonic airliners with improved operating efficiencies. Meanwhile, the primary vehicles for the U.S. carriers in the next decade would seem to be versions of current generation 747's, DC-10's, and the 1011's, along with their smaller subsonic brothers. There will be more of them as growth requires, and that growth will come.

4. Its Future Routes.

Over the past 50 years there have been hundreds of different airlines, just as there have been thousands of different railroads since the "iron horse" first came along. Many airlines have failed and folded, others have merged. United Airlines alone represents eight different carriers.

Today there are 11 U.S. trunk carriers (along with 8 regionals and a variety of "third level" operators), and a popular airline game is to guess how many there may be 10 years from now. One school suggests through merger and route swapping, there may be as few as five or six. Then there are those who believe the number may actually increase, as regionals may succeed in their attempts to expand into trunk status, and "third levelers" move up behind into new regionals, a cycle that has occurred in the past.

Here's what Carlson says on this subject:

"In times of financial distress there will always be pressures to consider mergers. On the other hand, if the airline industry is able to generate reasonable financial returns—somewhat consistent with what the CAB considers appropriate—then pressure for mergers is considerably less. And with the present public climate towards business, it would seem that pressures to resist corporate size will be increased. Thus for the next 5-10 years, I do not visualize any major mergers of carriers."

"Route-swapping" is a fairly new gambit which shows some promise, but not much in the way of results thus far. CAB spokesmen from time to time suggest this technique—airlines literally trading portions of their route structure with each other to reduce overcompetition and uneconomic service. The CAB may well encourage "route-swapping" provided public convenience is improved, or in any event not worsened.

One problem with "route-swapping" is that like horse-trading, it is difficult to find a situation wherein one carrier could trade a good route to another carrier for one of his good routes and each end up feeling completely satisfied. While United has no current "route-swapping" in its plans, conceivably this could alter its future system.

Still another factor is the CAB's perennial question as to how big is too big, or at least big enough. United as the largest trunk, with 23 percent of the total U.S. domestic market, is the Big Boy among the airlines, and as such cannot expect to be favored with much domestic route expansion.

There is one major route opportunity which could substantially change the future picture, and that is the Seattle/Tacoma-Tokyo-China application which United filed in early 1970. In the Transpacific Case decision, which denied United's application to Japan from California, the Seattle-Orient gateway question was left open by the CAB.

In many respects United would be the logical recipient of such an award if and when the CAB should bring that case through procedures to a decision. These reasons are stated in the company's application, and include the fact that with its coverage of U.S. markets to feed through the Seattle gateway, it could provide unparalleled public convenience. One of the more pragmatic arguments is that despite its size, United Airlines is the only U.S. domestic trunk carrier without any significant international route.

5. Its Future Service.

Since its inception, United has always represented the hallmark of good customer service. This philosophy remains basic to the company. It has used different ways to express the concept—"Extra Care," "Red Carpet," and others, but perhaps none has projected this thought to the public more effectively than "Fly the Friendly Skies of United."

Even so, with changing markets comes the need for changing services. At one time all air travel was "first class." Then coach was introduced in older and slower planes. Then coach and first-class compartments were provided on the same planes. First-class compartments had lounges; coach cabins did not. Today there are coach lounges, although perhaps not for long.

Out of every 100 air travelers today, 87 ride in coach. On Hawaii and Atlantic flights 96 of every 100 use coach or economy class. Both scheduled and supplemental airlines operate all-tourist charter flights.

In the future the airline must tailor its service to please the majority of its customers, and subordinate its past habit of overemphasizing deluxe service.

Chairman Timm of the CAB recently made an observation about elaborate in-flight service: "It seems to me that the airlines have been taking 'paupers' from the ground and treating them like 'princes' in the air, and in the process have risked reducing the airline industry to pauper status itself."

A single standard of service in the future? That's the way all airline service was before World War II and the postwar introduction of coach.

One type of in-flight accommodations? United tried that in 1963, and gave it up a year later when it failed.

A single-seating configuration in one aircraft? The Concorde will have 100 two-and-two coach-width seats.

"Air-bus" service? A negative merchandising term for what may possibly be tomorrow's in-flight standard.

Carlson sees the possibility of a single-class service sometime in the more distant future, with the exception of premium long-range schedules where, for an example, the main deck of a 747 would be coach throughout and the present upper lounge would be first class.

Whatever the service pattern of tomorrow, it must certainly be tailored and priced to please the great majority of the traveling public. This is how air transportation started out. This is how it succeeded, and this is how it will continue to succeed.

The key to good customer service is courtesy; it is the attitude and dedication of the women and men who serve the customer.

There are two concerns about future personnel throughout most service industries—the growing numbers of service personnel needed, and the changing attitudes of the younger generations. Here's what Carlson has to say on this subject:

"Insofar as the availability of satisfactory service personnel is concerned, I'm inclined to think that the airline employees who contact people will provide a more stabilized pool of personnel than other service industries. My reasoning is based upon the excellent salaries, benefits, and vacation privileges that flow with airline jobs, plus the pass privilege, which has to be one of the greatest employee benefits that goes to any employee in any industry. Attitudes are pretty much the responsibility of management. It is management's responsibility to indicate to all United employees (particularly 'public contact' employees) that they have a responsibility to the public. Attitudes are always difficult to shape, but I see no 'problems' that have not been a 'problem' during the past 30-40 years."

His observation is worth a second reading: "Attitudes are pretty much a responsibility of management."

This was Pat Patterson's guiding philosophy. This was the keystone he laid for United Airlines. It augurs well for the future United that Carlson lays out this guidepost for everyone.

6. Its Profitability.

Over the years United has generally been operated with efficiency, and with profitable results. It is a corporation staffed by employees, owned by stockholders, regulated by the government, to serve the traveling and shipping public. Much has been said by many people about the role of corporations, about the raison d'etre of the free enterprise system, about profits—and losses.

An interesting observation on the subject of corporations by John Steinbeck (an unusual observer to quote on this subject) is in his book, *America and Americans.* He said:

"Today, instead of the old, highly visible capitalist we have the corporation—one of the strangest organisms in the present world. It may manufacture goods for sale, operate mines, manipulate money, bore oil wells and crack the product into usable components, produce steel, copper, nickel, or tungsten, operate farms, or it may purchase the products of other corporations and distribute them; but its purpose is always to make money.

"The corporation, to exist at all, must be efficient, must produce its product or perform its function for a minimum of cost and a maximum of profit."[1]

There are those who argue that a corporation—particularly a service company such as United—does not exist for the purpose of making a profit, but rather, for the purpose of serving a consumer need, and that profits are a secondary consideration. That is a correct argument to this extent—unless a corporation satisfies a want, it will not long exist.

But unless a corporation makes a profit satisfying that want, it is certain to fail and disappear.

Profit is the foundation of the free enterprise system. It provides the means to furnish its service to the public, it provides wages and salaries to the employees, it provides dividends and investment growth to the stockholder, it provides funds to build and improve for the future, and it provides taxes for the support of governmental bodies.

The management of United places a very high priority on its objective to keep the company operating profitably in the future. Carlson has established as a corporate goal the achievement of a 12 percent R.O.I. or better on a regular year-in-and-year-out operating basis. This would be quite an achievement indeed, for it will be unprecedented among the major transcontinental trunk airlines; and such an achievement would more than safeguard United's position of industry leadership.

1. John Steinbeck, *America and the Americans* (New York: Viking Press, Inc., 1966).

7. Its Future Opportunities.

To the young man or woman in the company's lower or middle management ranks, there comes to mind the question: "Has this company matured and has its growth leveled off? Should I pursue my career with a company and in an industry which may be losing its dynamism?" The answer to that question has suggested itself in our look into United's future.

More to the point, in an organization this big, what opportunity does a young individual really have?

Here's Carlson's answer to that one:

"A very high priority in United Airlines' Five-Year Plan is the development of a management succession program. Much has been accomplished in this direction and the opportunities of surfacing and giving young men and women an opportunity for more responsibility is exciting.

"In addition to the other points concerning the advantages of the divisional concept, there is also the advantage of identifying a number of people who can assume major administrative positions in the divisions that might not have had an opportunity to function in a highly centralized organization. The decision was made sometime ago to move any man or woman who had the desire and the capability to take on more responsibilities, as rapidly as possible, across division lines, out of specialized functions into new administrative positions. The results have been encouraging. Granted, there have been some disappointments, but that's to be expected.

"This approach does give us the opportunity of identifying generalists as contrasted with specialists. The difference is substantial and necessary. The entrepreneur has always been a necessary part of the free-swinging, free enterprise system of this country. This means having confidence in yourself and putting at risk your own money or those that you report to with a conviction that your judgment will satisfy a market need and that the profits returned will be greater than the money put at risk. Sometimes the greater the risk, the greater the profits, and of course the failure. The larger the company and the more stilted the growth, the more difficult it is for the individual to take the entrepreneur risks that come with smaller companies or functioning as an individual. Consequently, oftentimes when a man meets the age when the decisions have to be made, he lacks the confidence to move ahead and make the management decisions or give the leadership necessary to have the company grow.

"Perhaps, under United's present organization, we can minimize the risks of on-the-job training and maximize at the right management age, the confidence necessary to be a good hard-nosed leader in the exciting days to come."

8. Its Future Freedom.

The growth of United Airlines in five short decades from zero to preeminence in transportation represents a classic case of free enterprise. To plan, to finance, to produce, and to market a wholly new service—to make that service an essential, well-accepted way of life—could only have been accomplished by entrepreneurial free enterprisers.

Yet United is not really free, and one of its challenges is to preserve the measure of freedom it has today.

Beginning with the Bureau of Aeronautics in 1926, United's routes and rates have been regulated by the federal government through a series of departments and bureaus, and its aircraft and operations also have been under the safety jurisdiction of federal authorities. Today there are essentially two agencies responsible for U.S. air transportation: the Civil Aeronautic Board, by law designated as an independent agency appointed by the Executive Branch to administer the route and rate affairs of the carriers, and the Federal Aviation Administration (and the independent Air Safety Board) under the Department of Transportation to function in the technological aspects of airways and aircraft.

These responsibilities are proper concerns of the federal government with its interstate responsibility. Nor is such supervision unique, for in transportation the Interstate Commerce Commission regulates railroads among other forms of surface transport, and the Federal Maritime Commission oversees our merchant marine. When one observes the endangered (and worsening) status of the rail and shipping industries, there is cause for concern about the future of the airlines—concern not just over the possibility of increasing government regulation, but concern over the possibility of nationalization of the industry.

There is reason for such concern because of events within the airline industry. From a legitimate regulation of rates and routes, the CAB has been gradually drawing closer to the board rooms and management tables of the carriers, involving itself in matters not specifically covered by the Act under which the CAB operates. They are small things, but symptomatic.

—Matters such as how many seats should be in an airplane and how far apart they should be spaced.

—Matters like whether liquor should be served at a charge, and if so, how much.

—Matters like how much an airline should pay an air traveler when he may be delayed for what period of time if his originally booked schedule is cancelled or otherwise does not accommodate him.

On occasion United has publicly challenged CAB actions it felt were improper and unwarranted. More recently the company has preferred to work out differences without public criticism, reasoning that the CAB and the carriers share responsibility for the industry, and in fact have a relationship as partners. Irrespective of the approach of confrontation or consultation, the effect has been about the same—a slow but steady movement toward government participation in management.

The real threat to airline management independence is not so much the unceasing series of specific nibbles; the danger lies in a continuation of the historic roller-coaster pattern of carrier profit and loss. A financially weak industry could be vulnerable to nationalization in one form or another—either outright, or by government's control of management actions. Either way, this would represent an incalculable defeat for United and for the industry, which prospect Carlson terms "simply horrible," and holds that it cannot be permitted to happen.

With the traditions of our nation solidly opposed to nationalization, with the CAB's present leadership outspoken for airline stability and strength, the prospect appears remote. But a resumption of large-scale losses by the industry, impairing operating capability and thwarting future capital requirements through inability to obtain finances, would quickly change the odds against survival of airline management freedom.

The needs of commerce, national defense and the public interest *require* air transportation regardless of economic considerations. If a financial catastrophe occurs, the government cannot permit airlines and other common carriers to close the doors as though they were ordinary business establishments. Then nationalization undoubtedly would be proposed as an answer.

How does Carlson view the future freedom of United and the industry? Here are his words:

"Airline managements, individually and collectively, fully recognize and actively assume responsibility for the future of the industry. Neither the government nor the financial community will ever replace effective managerial skills and energies as the first-line defense of free enterprise in air transportation. It is and it will be the job of airline management to preserve and to protect its present and future business independence. It can do this only by continuing to achieve profitable results from its operations; by maintaining efficiency, along with safety and dependability; by avoiding excesses in schedule capacities and in-service features; and by sticking to the business principle of giving the customer what he wants at the lowest price that will permit a reasonable profit.

"Our privately owned and operated air transport system has distinguished itself by its efficiency and low cost to the consumer; its development of new markets and classes of service; its improvements, innovations and technological advances; its safety and dependability record; and its ceaseless efforts to provide satisfaction for millions of customers.

"Despite its accomplishments, the system is vulnerable and its survival will depend on the collective wisdom of airline management, our regulators and others in government who share responsibility for what is now the finest air transport system in the world.

"The threads of possible change are there—they should be recognized and action initiated while there is still time."

For the action needed, Carlson has these priorities:

A national transportation plan—a key part of which is a logical basis for a sound airline route network and an optimum number of carriers provided on each major segment of that network.

A flexible system of airline pricing to match current rates with current costs; this would be a vital tool for airline management and the federal agency to help avoid perennial "yo-yo" profit and loss patterns.

A philosophy in government to permit airlines to earn the 12 percent rate of return found by the CAB to be reasonable and proper.

A dedicated determination on the part of United's entire organization to fulfill its primary responsibility of operating effectively and profitably, to preserve and extend the company's stability and integrity.

Carlson sums up United's future this way:

"The growth of the airline industry in the past 50 years has been exciting. There is no reason to believe the next 50 years will not be equally exciting."

You can be sure that Eddie Carlson is doing a great deal to make it so.

Epilogue

I n 1934, *United's Rule of Three was Safety, Passenger Comfort, Dependability.*

In 1954, United's Rule of Five was Safety, Service, Dependability, Honesty, Sincerity.

In 1974, United's Rule of Five had become Safety, Service, Profitability, Integrity, Responsibility. These would be the guideposts for the company's move into the future.

United Airlines will celebrate its 50th anniversary in 1976, the nation's bicentennial year. It will be evident that most of the 200-year development of America has occurred during the last half-century. From the birth of our nation, transportation has been the main artery of growth, and it is no coincidence that the United States achieved a truly national status when air transportation came to dominate common carrier passenger transport.

What about the year 2026—the end of the next 50 years? Or even 2001, when United Airlines should observe its 75th birthday?

With no practicable new technology to replace its present vehicles, with a few signs that its growth curve may be flattening, is air transportation reaching its full maturity?

As cities grow into metropolises, as metropolises merge into megalopolises, and then as present life-styles are replaced by new ones, what will happen to the present air-travel markets? Will they grow, or shrink, or dis-

201

appear, or will they develop new and different patterns?

Will there be a United Airlines in 2026, or even 2001?

If man can make exploration of the moon common-place in a few short years, what will travel in the United States, or around the world — or to the stars — be like in the next 50 years, or even the next 25? Will there be supersonic airliners at Mach 3? Or rockets at Mach 7? Or some other as yet undreamed-of vehicle?

No engineer developing future technology will determine the life span of United Airlines. The answer will come from the men and women now in United, and from the others who will follow them in years to come.

But the answer can be "yes" only if those who have today's management responsibilities fulfill their trust, and build for tomorrow as well as or better than their predecessors built for today.

Then there can and there will be a United Airlines in the year 2001, and in 2026, and beyond.

Acknowledgments

The author wishes to thank the following publishers for permission to reprint excerpts from their works:

"What's Wrong with the Airlines," *Fortune* (August, 1946). Michael B. Rothfeld, "New Downdrafts for the Airlines," *Fortune* (January, 1974). Rush Loving Jr., "How a Hotelman Got the Red out of United Air Lines," *Fortune* (March, 1972).

John Steinbeck, *America and the Americans* (New York: Viking Press, Inc., 1966).

Frank J. Taylor, *Pat Patterson*. Reprinted by permission of Lane Magazine and Book Company.

Index